Kings Poole
Meeds

23

Sowe flu.

1 Graye fri
2 Foregate s
3 Pinfolde
4 North gat
5 Crabery la
6 S. Chads Chur:
7 S. Maryes chu:
8 FreeSchole
9 Tipping stret
10 House of Correct
11 Dottell prick
12 Broade eye
13 New bridge
14 Tanter bank
15 Castle hill
16 Mill gate
17 Earles stret
18 South gate
19 Martins lane
20 Saltars stret
21 Almeshouse la:
22 Eastgate stret
23 East gate
24 Beire lane
25 Church lane
26 Mill lane
27 Highe stret
28 Shire hall
29 Forebridge
30 Stafford.

Yesterday's Town: Stafford 1984
has been published as a Limited
Edition of which this is

Number   12

A complete list of the original
subscribers is printed at the
back of the book

Kind Regards

[signature]

YESTERDAY'S TOWN: STAFFORD

FRONT COVER: Stafford Railway Station (1841). (WSL)

The Ancient High House. (WSL)

YESTERDAY'S TOWN:
STAFFORD

BY

PAUL BUTTERS

BARRACUDA BOOKS LIMITED
BUCKINGHAM, ENGLAND
MCMLXXXIV

PUBLISHED BY BARRACUDA BOOKS LIMITED
BUCKINGHAM, ENGLAND
AND PRINTED BY
BUSIPRINT LIMITED
BUCKINGHAM, ENGLAND

BOUND BY
GREEN STREET BINDERY LIMITED
OXFORD, ENGLAND

JACKET PRINTED BY
CHENEY & SONS LIMITED
BANBURY, OXON

LITHOGRAPHY BY
M.R.M. GRAPHICS LIMITED
WINSLOW, ENGLAND

DISPLAY SET IN TIMES
AND TEXT SET IN 12/13 TIMES ROMAN BY
GECKO LIMITED
BICESTER, OXON

© Paul Butters 1984

ISBN 0 86023 194 1

CONTENTS

KEY TO CAPTION CREDITS

B Sch	Brooklands School	SIGS	Stafford Independent Grammar School
Mrs Dy	Mrs Dymott	SN	*Stafford Newsletter*
Mrs Dav	Mrs Davies	SCC	Stafford Cricket Club
TB	Mr Tony Bloor	SHC	Stafford Hockey Club
CE	Mr C. Ecclestone	SRUFC	Stafford Rugby Union FC
ES	*Evening Sentinel*	SJT	Mr S.J. Timmins
E&S	*Express and Star*	SCCM	Staffs County Council Museum (Shugborough)
EH	Mr E Haywood	SCCD	Staffs County Council, Planning and
KEHS	King Edward VI High School		Development Dept.
PR	Peter Rogers	SS	Mrs S. Simpson
Mrs M	Mrs Mottershead	JW	Mr John Whitehouse
PN	Mr P Newbold	St J's C	St Joseph's Convent
WSL	William Salt Library	RCP	Mr R.C. Pepper
Mrs S	Mrs Sherratt	HV	Henry Venables Ltd
BS	Bertram Sinkinson	SV	Mr Sidney Venables
SH & CS	Stafford Historical and Civic Society	MS	Mr Michael Smethurst

ACKNOWLEDGEMENTS

However modest its aims, it would be impossible to produce a book of this kind without the assistance of others more knowledgeable than oneself. My particular thanks are due to Mr Douglas Johnson, assistant editor of *The Victorian History of the County of Stafford*, for the time and trouble he has taken in reading the script and, inevitably, improving it; to Dr C. G. Gilmore who has given me his assistance, especially with the chapter on education; to Sister Angela for photographs of and information about St Joseph's Convent School; to Mr Fred Stitt, the County Archivist, and the staff of the William Salt Library, for their usual invaluable help; and to Mrs Shirley Simpson for her advice about the Staffordshire Bull Terrier. My thanks also to the proprietors of *The Stafford Newsletter* and *The Staffordshire Advertiser* who have again allowed me access to old copies of their newspapers: all the press quotes come from these invaluable sources.

This is my second book about my native town, and it differs in one respect from the first: in *Stafford: The Story of a Thousand Years*, the illustrations were secondary to the text; in the present book the order has, to some extent, been reversed, a change which some will no doubt consider an improvement. While actual repetition has been reduced to a minimum, some reference has had to be made to the material contained in the original book to complete a coherent story of the county town. The present one has enabled me not only to bring that story up-to-date (particularly the sporting scene, which changes almost from year to year), but also to deal with new subjects which it was not possible, through lack of space, to include in the original work.

To provide the necessary illustrations promised to be a formidable task, and I am grateful to all those people who have supplied me with photographs. I am particularly indebted, in that respect, to Mr Roy Lewis, the County Inspector for History, assistant archivist, Mrs Joan Anslow, and the William Salt Library who have together placed an enormous amount of slides and prints at my disposal. My thanks also to Mr David Slee, SCC Assistant County Planning and Development Officer, for scenic photographs, and to Mr Anthony Rogers for his professional assistance in the preparation of many of the pictures, which I hope will leaven any shortcomings in the text for which I have to accept full responsibility.

P.B. 1984.

YESTERDAY'S TOWN

One of the solaces of old age is to recall the days of one's youth, and Staffordians of my generation have much to remember about their native town: the horse-drawn cabs, patiently awaiting a fare outside the railway station; the cries of 'Whip behind!' to warn the driver that some intrepid youngster is clinging precariously to the back of his vehicle, enjoying a free ride; the lamplighter making his round of the gaslit streets, shouldering his long pole like Albert's musket; the metallic clang of the blacksmith's hammer and the acrid smell of his forge; Guisso's icecream cart, with its penny cornets and twopenny wafers; the Italian organgrinder, his monkey perched on his shoulder, raising its red fez when the music changed; the German Band, which disappeared on the outbreak of the First World War; Gustav Hamel (later reputed to be a Germany spy, when there was one under every bed) and his 'Thrilling Flying Exhibition' on the Common; the milk float, like a Roman chariot which Ben Hur might have driven, laden with churns to fill the jugs left on doorsteps, beaded protective nets over them; the three brass balls of the pawnshop; picnics at Tinkerborough and Shaky Bridges (where the bridges really *did* shake); band concerts in Victoria Park, and the amusement fair in the Market Square, which I remember with particular affection. I spent many an exciting Saturday morning, perched on the Victorian drinking fountain, watching the swings and roundabouts being erected and listening to the patter of the cheapjacks, with an occasional interruption from the Salvation Army Band, whose headquarters were in a room over the Penny Bazaar in Crabbery Street.

Since then, time and the Industrial Revolution have wrought many changes. The conversion of a quiet market town into a sprawling industrial city began 200 years ago, when William Horton opened his boot and shoe factory in Mill Street in the late 1700s. After the enclosure of Foregate field in 1807, the footwear industry became concentrated in the north end of the town, where there was a rapid increase in population and new streets were laid out and houses built to accommodate the workers. The name of Stafford was to be synonymous with the boot and shoe trade until well into the present century, but new industries had begun to trespass on the scene by the mid-1800s, many of them starting as ancillaries of the footwear industry before seeking wider horizons. Ironically, they were to be responsible for its gradual decline: in 1851, there were 29 boot and shoe manufacturers in the town: today, there is only one — Lotus Ltd, founded in 1822 by Thomas Bostock as a small family business, which was to grow into one of the largest of its kind in the world.

As industry grew, so did the town and its environs. Castletown (also known as Newtown) developed round the railway station when it was built in 1837, and was further extended when Venables Saw Mills opened in Doxey Road in 1864, to be followed, 12 years later, by the Castle Engine Works of W.G. Bagnall, the locomotive builders. Victoria Road, leading from the Station to the town, was built in 1866, a bridge was constructed over the river and the streets adjoining St Mary's Church opened up to create Victoria Square, where the Technical School was built in 1896. When most of Coton Field was enclosed in 1880, the area was developed as a residential district and a school was built at Littleworth. Crooked Bridge Road, the old access road from Foregate, was extended to join Coton Field, and Corporation Street was constructed in the mid-1890s. (This already long road was to be extended still further in 1914, when Riverway was completed, and continued it across the river to Lichfield Road.) What was to become a well known local landmark appeared in the main street when the Brine Baths were built by the river in 1892; by the end of the century the town had assumed what was to be a familiar shape until the planners got to work on it in the 1970s.

In the meantime, W.H. Dorman & Co, whose diesel engines were later to command a world market, had come upon the scene in 1870, and salt production was started in 1887 when, quite by chance, brine was discovered during borings on the Common by the Corporation, in search of pure water. The Town's industrial growth was reflected in the increase of its population. When Horton opened his factory, it numbered less than 4,000; when Siemens opened theirs, 100 years later, it had grown to more than 20,000. Siemens Bros, of Woolwich, a German firm, was to revolutionise the industrial scene when it opened its factory in Lichfield Road in 1903, and built an estate at Stychfields (known to the locals as 'Siemens Colony') to accommodate a workforce which was soon to become by far the largest in the town. Siemens heavy electric engineering business was purchased by the English Electric Co in 1919; Dormans and Bagnalls were taken over in 1961; and in 1968 the EEC merged with the General Electric Co to become the mammoth GEC. It is often asked why Siemens chose Stafford as their centre. No doubt the answer is that they opened their main factory in the county town for the same reason that King Alfred's daughter, Ethelfleda, had established her defensive 'burgh' there 1,000 years earlier: its central geographical position, with road junctions providing access to all parts of the country.

A remarkable feature of the town's industrial growth was its parochial origin: major companies like Lotus, Dormans, Bagnalls, Venables and others, were all founded by local men. The same can be said of its trade. I can remember when nearly all the main street shops were privately owned, most of them by locals. I have before me a list of the shops of 1912, which will have a familiar ring for older Staffordians: Martin Mitchell, the Great Cycle Expert; Miss Bell's Artistic Millinery; the Zetland Tea Rooms (the Café Royal); Cowleys, the tailors; Woodalls, the drapers; T.A. Dunn, the clothier; F. Pickering, the artificial teeth maker; Dales and Thornes, the ironmongers; Harry Mercer, the saddler; Arthur Dobson, the tobacconist; Averills and Fowkes, the chemists; Mottrams and Smethursts, the jewellers; the Maypole Dairy . . . these are just a few of an endless catalogue of names to whet the elderly appetite.

But that was yesterday.

Today, the industrial field has grown even wider, with major companies like the Universal Grinding Wheel (1913), the British Reinforced Concrete (1926) and Evode, the adhesives manufacturers, added to an already impressive list, and the establishment of a large industrial estate on land between the Sandon and Common Roads in the 1970s. But nowhere is the change in the character of the town more apparent than in the make-up of its main street. When the Brine Baths were demolished in 1977, to be replaced by the Civic Offices, nearly all the cosy little shops of 70 years ago had already disappeared and given way to a street of supermarkets, banks, building societies, insurance companies and the like. A few familiar names like Mottrams, Woodalls and T.A. Dunn have defied the wind of change, but only one family business, as such, survives: Michael Smethurst, the present proprietor, still carries on the jewellery business which his forbears founded in 1860.

Greengate Street (c1858).
(WSL)

ABOVE: Ancient High House (c1825). (SJT)   BELOW: Green Bridge (c1860). (WSL)

12

LEFT: South of Green Bridge (c1860). RIGHT: The mill. (WSL) BELOW: An unfamiliar view of the Market Square (c1895).

ABOVE: Market Square with bandstand and Victorian drinking fountain (c1905). (WSL)
BELOW: Old boathouse on the site of which the Brine Baths were built in 1892. (SH&CS)

14

ABOVE: A view of the old town from Newport Road, with St Mary's Church and the mill in the background (c1840). (SH&CS) BELOW: Gaol Square (c1906), with the old cast iron gentlemen's convenience to the right of the fountain. The Abercrombie Inn and one of the towers of the prison in Gaol Road can be seen in the background. (KE – HS)

LEFT: Church Lane (c1840). (WSL) BELOW: Church Lane (c1906). (SH&CS) RIGHT: Primrose Cottage (1610), now the County Fruit stores, in Mill Street, (WSL)

ABOVE: The Post Office and Boot's the chemist's, in Market Square (c1910). BELOW: Cabbies awaiting a fare outside the railway station (c1905). (PR)

ABOVE: Emmanuel Guisso, ice cream vendor, taking delivery of a load of ice (c1905). (CE)
CENTRE: Gustav Hamel's 'thrilling flying exhibition' on Stone Road Common (1913). (SCCM)
BELOW: The original Lichfield Road factory, opened in 1903 by Siemen's Bros, the German electric engineering company which was to revolutionise the local industrial scene when it was taken over in 1919 by the English Electric Co, and finally merged with the mammoth General Electric Co in 1968.

18

Tinkerborough, the picnicker's paradise.

ABOVE: A 1920 milk float. (SCCM) BELOW: Victoria Park, before it was extended to the other side of the river in 1910. In the background, to the left, can be seen the bandstand where Sunday Concerts were a popular feature.

ABOVE: The Amusement Fair in the cobble-stoned Market Square, another popular event before the 1914–18 War. (WSL) LEFT: The ruins of Lotus factory (affectionately known as 'Bostock's shoe factory') after its destruction by fire in 1901. The new factory in Sandon Road was opened two years later. (RCP) RIGHT: Salt workers. (WSL)

21

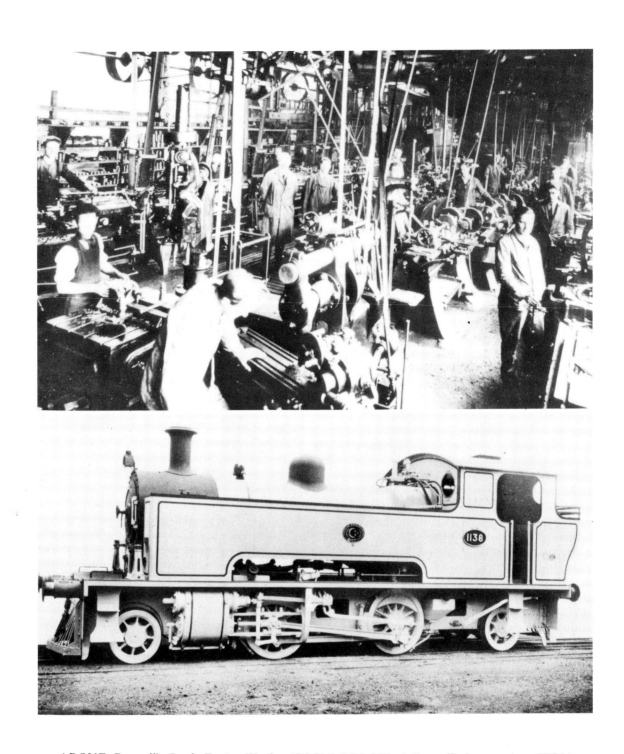

ABOVE: Bagnall's Castle Engine Works. (SCCM) BELOW: A Bagnall's locomotive. (WSL)

ABOVE: Venables Saw Mills (1975). (HV) BELOW: Venables 'trimming out', Bagot Park (1933). (HV)

Martin Mitchell, The Great Cycle Expert.

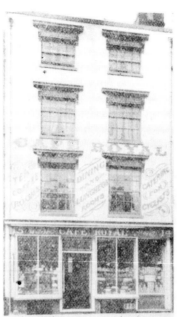

A few of the host of main street premises which have disappeared from the scene.

ABOVE: The Cafe Royal; RIGHT: Miss Bell's the milliners; BELOW: Dale's the ironmongers. (WSL)

LEFT: Averill's the chemist's; RIGHT: Turner & Co, the outfitters; BELOW: Brookfields, the drapers and furnishers.

ABOVE: The original premises of Smethurst's the jewellers, established in 1860, the only family business to survive, as such; (Mr Michael Smethurst in the foreground). (MS) BELOW: The present premises, on the other side of Greengate Street. (MS)

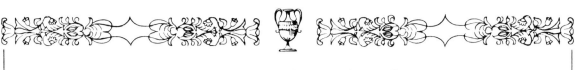

THE BEGINNING

To the stranger, the mention of Staffordshire immediately conjures up a picture of an ugly, heavily industrialised district, with coal mines and iron foundries, blast furnaces and slagheaps; and the approach to the Potteries like a journey into Hades, the road flanked by potbanks and bottle ovens, flames belching from the furnaces. Nothing could be further from the truth. Apart from the fact that modern systems, like the firing of the kilns by gas and electricity, have improved the appearance of its industrial belt, Staffordshire has always had a wealth of rich agricultural land, and scenery as beautiful and varied as any to be found in the more fashionable counties.

Stafford has been as much misunderstood as the county it represents: it is not, and never has been, part of the Black Country or the Potteries. A good fifteen miles away from both, the town into which I was born in the first decade of the century was a comfortable little place, well satisfied with itself, slow to accept new ideas and suspicious of strangers — in fact, a typical county town. The encroachment of industry (with some assistance from the town planners) has changed all that; but although the pleasant market town, nestling quietly in its agricultural cocoon, has given way to a much less attractive industrial centre, the adjoining countryside has remained largely unspoilt, and a number of delightful villages can still be found within a few miles of the town centre: Haughton, 'the village in the meadows', with its Old Hall, dating from the Reformation; Gnosall, with its fine Parish Church and its ancient lock-up, a carbon copy of the one in Stafford's Lichfield Road; Eccleshall (a small market town now, rather than a village) with its 13th century church and its Castle, the principal residence of the Bishops of Lichfield for more than five hundred years until 1878, which resisted a siege by the Parliamentary forces during the Civil War longer than did its counterpart in Stafford; and the village of Milford, the gateway to the wild beauty of Cannock Chase, once a great oak forest, the pleasure ground of kings, two thousand acres of which were donated to the Staffordshire County Council by the Earl of Lichfield, in 1956.

Like other county towns, Stafford is steeped in history. It is said that St Bertelin, a Mercian Prince, established a hermitage on what was then an island called Bethnei, in the marshes of the Sow, c700; two centuries later, legend gave way to fact when King Alfred's martial daughter, Ethelfleda, put Stafford in the history books for the first time, building her defensive 'burh' there in 913, during her campaign against the Danes. The Millenary Pageant, to celebrate that historic event, is one of the first things I remember about my native town. Held in Castle Fields on Saturday and Monday, 2 and 4 August 1913, the site originally proposed had been Stafford Rangers football ground, but the organisers had a change of mind and finally decided that the fields adjoining the Castle would be a more appropriate venue. It was a popular — indeed, an obvious — choice, but the selection of events was a different matter. The story of the county town had been a long and turbulent one, and the organising committee had an embarrassing surfeit of material at its disposal: its problem was not so much what to include in its programme as what it dared leave out. The Norman Conquest and its aftermath, when William ruthlessly suppressed a rebellion and defeated the Saxon forces, led by Edric the Wild, at the battle of Stafford in 1069; Richmond's meeting with Stanley on his way to Bosworth and the defeat of Richard III; the imprisonment of Mary, Queen of Scots, at Chartley, in 1586; the regicide, John Bradshaw (elected MP for Stafford in 1654) presiding at the trial of Charles I and signing his death warrant; the 'forty-five' rebellion, when 'Butcher' Cumberland dined at Chetwynd House before joining General Wade at Stone and halting the Young Pretender's drive to London . . . these are but a few fragments of local history, taken at random, which had to be omitted. The organisers had a difficult task, but no one could really complain about their final choice.

Of the seven episodes they selected, the first two were as inevitable as Greek drama; a soliloquy by Bertelin, the town's patron saint, delivered by Mr Percy Edgar, who 'displayed his elocutionary powers to great advantage', was followed by Ethelfleda (Miss Nora Knight), dressed in a purple gown trimmed with gold, and mounted on 'a fine grey steed', announcing, to thunderous applause, the defeat of 'the heathen Dane'. Episode three (in which the Rector of St Mary's, Rev Lionel Lambert played Father Francis 'with becoming dignity') featured the arrival of a King's Messenger in the Market Square, bearing King John's Charter of Liberties. Episode four starred a weary Richard II, escorted through the town by the usurper, Bolingbroke, seeking permission to dismount and rest awhile, a part played by Mr A. Garner, 'whose exposition could not have been excelled'. Two hundred extras appeared in the next epic, the visit of Elizabeth I in 1575, a rôle sustained 'with queenly grace and dignity' by Mrs E. Buckhardt, William Lamb, the schoolmaster who welcomed her at the East Gate being played, appropriately enough, by Mr E.O. Powell, the headmaster of the Grammar School. The Civil War battle of Hopton Heath came next, the Earl of Northampton dying a hero's death, defying the rebels and refusing quarter — 'I scorn your quarter, base rogues and rebels as you are'. The final episode dealt with the first of the notorious 'bribery and corruption' elections. (Stafford narrowly escaped disenfranchisement in 1837, when the writ for its right to the two members it had returned since the reign of Edward I scraped through Parliament by a single vote.) This particular episode concerned the 1780 election, when Richard Brinsley Sheridan took time off from his Drury Lane Theatre to buy sufficient votes to ensure a seat which he was to hold for the next twenty-six years.

Whether or not the actors were as good as the press would have us believe, the Millenary Pageant was a remarkable feat of organisation. All the episodes were prepared by local people, many of the costumes made and designed by the Stafford School of Art, and nearly a thousand amateur players (not to mention forty horses) took part in an enterprise which deserves its own modest niche in the town's story. There was some disappointment when the Castle itself was not included, but the truth was that the organisers would have been hard pressed to find much of interest to say about it. Originally built as a stately home for the descendants of the Norman overlord, Robert de Toeni, it was not until it was rebuilt in the 1350s by the first Earl of Stafford that it could be called a castle, with its battlements and towers; and when it was again rebuilt, c1800 by George, the son of Sir William Jerningham, the work was never properly finished and, although the structure looked impressive silhouetted against the sky, it was little more than a theatrical showpiece. The only castle designed to be used as a fortress had been built by William the Conqueror in 1070 — probably in the Broad Eye area — following the rebellion of the previous year. It never had to be used in defence of the Norman occupation, was allowed to fall into decay and was in ruins by 1086, the date of Domesday Book.

Ethelfleda's is not the only famous name which Stafford can claim. Edmund Stafford, the founder of Exeter College, Oxford, was born at the Castle in the mid-1300s. Bishop of Exeter in the reign of Richard II, and Henry IV's Lord High Chamberlain, he ended a distinguished career as Archbishop of York. John Stafford, a Franciscan Friar and a member of the same family, surely has a claim to fame, if only because he wrote a history of England, c1380 — in Latin, as most histories were at that time. Three Staffordians became Lord Mayor of London — Sir Thomas Offley in 1556–7, Sir Hugh Homersley in 1627–8 and Thomas Sidney in 1853–4 — but Izaac Walton remains the best known of all the town's sons. Born on 9 August 1593 and baptised at St Mary's on 21 September, the author of *The Compleat Angler* died at Winchester on 15 December 1683, and was buried in the Cathedral. A plaque on the wall of the new Police Station in Eastgate Street indicates the site of the cottage where he is said to have been born. In the realm of the arts, John Prescott Knight, RA (1803–1881), the son of the celebrated comedian, Edward Knight (who performed at the Martin Street theatre from 1799 to 1802), achieved fame as a portrait painter; and while William Congreve, the Restoration dramatist — described as 'the greatest English dramatist of pure comedy', though one wonders whether 'pure' is the right word — was not a native of the town, he had close connections with it. His father lived at Congreve Manor, near Penkridge, and his famous son spent quite a lot of time in the district.

In more recent times, the name of Congreve has brought honour to the town in an entirely different context. Captain (later General Sir Walter) Congreve won the Victoria Cross in South Africa on 15 December 1899; and when his son, Major William Congreve, was awarded the same decoration in the First World War, the Congreves became only the third father and son to win this, the highest military honour for gallantry in the field. Major Congreve was one of the country's most highly decorated soldiers, his medals for gallantry including the DSO and the MC as well as his posthumous VC, awarded after he was killed at Longueval on the Somme, in July 1916.

Though most of the town's history has been lost in the mists of time, a few reminders still remained when the Millenary Pageant was over. The demolition of buildings adjoining the Coach and Horses Inn in Mill Bank disclosed that the existing walls had been built onto the lower courses of the old stone ones, which had replaced Ethelfleda's primitive defences; another stretch of the old walls could still be seen in North Walls in the 1920s, while part of the East Gate, at the junction with Lammascote Road, survives to this day. When it was dismantled in 1800, part of it was left standing and, when road widening in 1939 threatened to complete its destruction, it was decided that this relic of the old town should be preserved and it was removed and re-erected nearby, where it still stands, a grim reminder of the past.

Stafford appears in Domesday Book as the chief town of Staffordshire: in fact, it was already the administrative centre of the county in the 10th century, with a Royal Mint where coins were struck from the reign of Athelstan (924–939) until that of Henry II (1154–89). Another link with royalty was the King's Pool, a stretch of water covering the land between the East Gate and what is now Corporation Street. The fish pool was in existence in the 1150s, when it also formed part of the town's defences. The Sheriff was responsible for fishing the pool on behalf of the King, providing him with bream, pike and tench and, in 1253, he was ordered to sell the fish in the pool except 'the little fish called frit'. Custody of the pool was first granted to William, son of Wymer, and his heirs, in 1197–98, at a rent of ½ mark; and in his *Handbook and Guide to Stafford*, a more knowledgeable and informative little book than its modest title suggests, Cecil Hibbert refers to a document in the Harleian Collection which sets out the conditions on which it was being held by Ralph de Wymer in 1273: 'That when the king should please to fish, he was to have the pikes and breams, and the said Ralph and his heirs were to have all the other fishes, with the eels, coming to the hooks, rendering therefor to the king half a mark at the Feast of St Michael.' Hibbert also mentions '. . . an ancient Roll [which] gives particulars of payments made in 1281 for fishing in "the lake at Stafford" and sending the catch to Rhuddlan Castle for the use of the Queen of Edward I'. The pool had disappeared by 1606, but the site was subject to flooding in bad weather, and it temporarily resumed its original role during the Civil War, when the area was flooded artificially by the Parliamentary committee, as a defensive measure.

The right to hold a market — ie 'to sell goods in the open and along the public thoroughfare' — was first granted by King John's charter of 1206, and the cobblestoned Market Square, with its Market Cross, was the focal point of local trade for centuries. The ground floor of the Elizabethan Town Hall — 'a fayre hall, all built with free stone, very high and stately' — was used as a market from the late 16th century until 1798, when it was replaced by the present Shire Hall. Two years later the erection of a small building at the rear of the new hall, for the sale of farm produce, heralded the gradual erosion of the open air market. When the Guildhall was built, across the road, in 1853–54, another market hall was erected behind it and more stalls were transferred to the covered accommodation; but it was not until 1927 that the few remaining were finally dismantled and removed to the present St John's Market Hall. As well as the Market Cross, the Square housed the stocks and the pillory, where minor offenders served as human Aunt Sallies for those who had nothing better to do than shower them with rotten eggs and decaying vegetables. A Russian cannon, captured at Sebastopol, was displayed there in 1869, before being moved to Pitcher Bank, and I can remember the tank which went on show to promote the sale of Savings Certificates during the First World War.

Stafford has always owed a lot to its central geographical position. As a consequence, the coach trade flourished until the coming of the railway, and the postilion, on entering the town, would drive his coach through the Green Bridge boatyard to wash away the mud and dust of his journey in the river which ran alongside it. In 1765, four-wheeled chaises could be hired at the Saracen's Head in the Market Square, and by the late 1790s the town was on the daily route to London, Chester, Birmingham and Manchester. Weekly coaches started for London and Birmingham from the Star and the George on the west side of the Square, and the Swan and the Bear in Greengate Street.

While providing plenty of excitement for those who had never seen a train, the opening of the Grand Junction Railway in 1837 had a disastrous effect on the business of the coaching inns. 'We do not hear that there will be a Festival of any kind on this occasion', *The Staffordshire Advertiser* reported on 1 July 1837. 'Many, if not all, the coaches between Birmingham and Manchester will be taken off the road'. The next edition described the euphoric effect of the advent of the railway. The arrival of the first train was greeted with a salute of 21 guns, and 'the amazement of those who had never before witnessed railroad travelling was indescribable. Time', it added, reassuringly if not prophetically, 'was toleraby well kept'. Thereafter, the railway prospered to such an extent that, within seven years, a new station had to be built to meet the demand of this new and exciting form of travel. Designed by John Cunningham, of Liverpool, the new building, with its Elizabethan style of architecture, 'adapted for the purposes of one of the greatest modern inventions [was] considered to be the most commodious and complete station in the line between London and Liverpool'. (*The Staffordshire Advertiser*, 2 March 1844.) Faced with the inevitable, the coaching inns accepted defeat with a good grace. 'A handsome omnibus' was run by a Mr Meeson from the Swan to the railway station, while others were soon covering a wider area. The new station was itself rebuilt on a larger scale in 1861–2, and the North Western Hotel was erected, across the road, four years later. Affectionately remembered as the Station Hotel (a favourite rendezvous of the lawyers at Assize time), it became one of the planners' principal victims when it was demolished in 1972.

For a town of such increasing importance, it is difficult to realise how small Stafford had always been. When William suppressed the 1069 rebellion, it had been laid waste, a third of its dwellings were destroyed and only some 600 inhabitants survived the slaughter. By the time of the Civil War, their number had increased by no more than 1,000, and at the beginning of the 19th century the first national census returned a figure of 3,898 as the local population, which meant that there had been an increase of little more than 3,000 in almost 750 years. Then came the Industrial Revolution and a dramatic change: by the 1890s the population exceeded 20,000.

Some examples of Staffordshire scenic beauty. ABOVE LEFT: Brocton Coppice, Cannock Chase; RIGHT: 'The Vista Seat', Kinver Edge; BELOW LEFT: Consall Forge, and canal pleasure boats; RIGHT: the Manifold Valley and Thor's Cave. (All SCCD)

LEFT: Eccleshall High Street. (PR) RIGHT: Chetwynd House, a favourite rendezvous of R.B. Sheridan and William Horton, the pioneer of the boot and shoe trade. Sheridan is said to have written The School for Scandal *in one of its rooms. (WSL) BELOW: Opening of Chetwynd House as the Post Office in 1914.*

*Stafford Millenary Pageant, 1913: ABOVE:
clergy in Chapter Scene. (E.O. Powell, centre.)
(JW) BELOW: Sheridan Election scene. (SV)*

ABOVE LEFT: St Bertelin (Mr P. Edgar);
(JW) RIGHT; Richard II (Mr A Garner); (JW)
BELOW LEFT: Ethelfleda (Miss Nora
Knight); and RIGHT: Elizabeth I (Mrs E.
Buckhardt). (JW)

ABOVE LEFT: Stafford Castle in the 1870s, and RIGHT: in the 1950s. (WSL) BELOW LEFT: Bust of Izaak Walton in St Mary's Church; RIGHT: coach house and stable in Eastgate Street (c1880), reputed formerly to have been the cottage where he was born in 1593, and OPPOSITE ABOVE: his cottage at Shallowford. ('ES') Remnants of the old town walls: BELOW: in Mill Bank, uncovered during demolition work in 1926. (SH&CS)

LEFT: The old walls at the Mount, off Gaol Square, (SH&CS) BELOW: Thieves' Ditch, North Walls, (SH&CS); RIGHT: part of the East Gate wall, removed and preserved after road widening in 1939. (SH&CS)

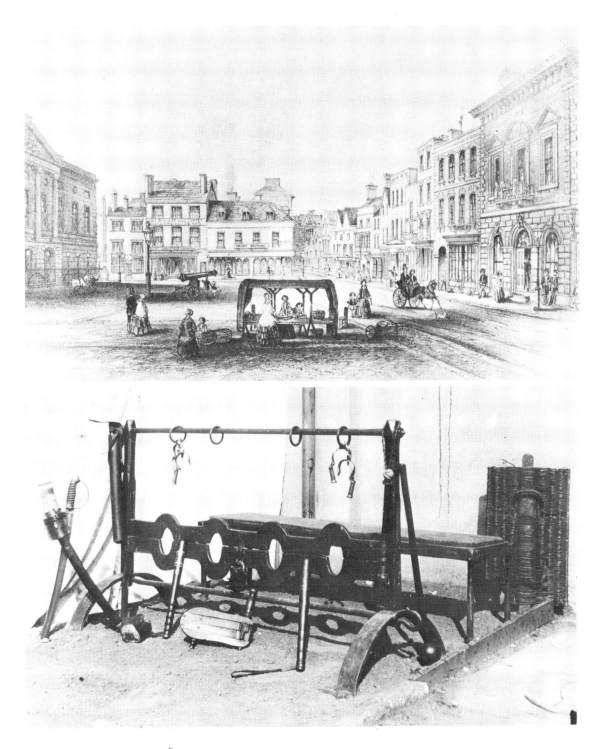

ABOVE: The Market Square (c1860), (SJT) and BELOW: the stocks, originally in Market Square. (WSL)

OPPOSITE ABOVE: Volunteers on the outbreak of 1914–18 war, (BS) and BELOW: final parade of the New Zealand Rifle Brigade (stationed at Brocton), May, 1919. (BS) ABOVE: Approach to the railway station (1841). (WSL) BELOW: Arrival of wounded during 1914–18 war.

The opening of the Grand Junction Railway – 'one of the greatest modern inventions' (vide press) in 1837, was greeted with a salute of 21 guns. ABOVE: A railway accident (1906). (WSL) BELOW: The Station Hotel (1910).

THE GOOD — AND THE BAD
— OLD SPORTING DAYS

Although Stafford's industrial and business growth had been satisfactory enough, its cultural progress left much to be desired. The little theatre in Martin Street was always fighting a losing battle and, though sport really was sport and not the big business it is today, it also had its dark corners, as we shall see. Staffordians of the 18th and 19th centuries enjoyed one sport which we are denied today. Race meetings were held, first at Coton Fields in the 1790s, and later, from 1820, on a new course at Stone Road Common; but, like the theatre, it was always on a knife-edge of failure. Apart from taking Harriot Mellon, the future Duchess of St Albans, from the obscurity of the Martin Street playhouse to the bright lights of Drury Lane, R.B. Sheridan's contribution to the local theatre was negligible; but he was prepared to lose money on the race course as readily as he did at Drury Lane, and helped to infuse some life into a dying sport when he persuaded the Prince Regent to attend a meeting in 1790. After Sheridan, Joshua Drewry, who founded *The Staffordshire Advertiser*, the town's first weekly newspaper, in 1795, took up the cudgels. With his journalistic flair for publicity, he managed to postpone the inevitable for a few more years, but the end came when the course was closed in 1847.

Though there was to be no more horseracing after 1847, there was plenty of other sport available. The first reference in the press to a cricket club came in that same year when on Saturday, 10 July, *The Staffordshire Advertiser* announced that a cricket match, Stafford *v* Trentham, was to be played at Trentham Park on the following Monday, and 'should the weather prove fine, a large company will no doubt assemble to witness the sport'. This early team was probably a nomadic side, with no regular fixture list, and it was not until 17 years later that a public meeting was called 'for the purpose of establishing a cricket club in the town'; the club was formally constituted, officers were appointed and the Mayor, Mr J. Pilling, became its first President. (*The Staffordshire Advertiser* 9 April 1864.)

Like most spectator sports, cricket was first played on the Lammascotes, and it was there that a memorable game was played against Burton on 10 August 1889 — memorable because the visitors included in their side F.R. Spofforth, the Australian 'demon bowler' who had created the mythical Ashes when he destroyed the English batting at the Oval in 1882. 'The demon' had played his last Test Match against England only two years before his appearance at Stafford, and it was not surprising that the committee should strengthen their side by including five professionals. No doubt the five amateurs they replaced were not too pleased with this extravagance, but they had the last laugh. The pros did not enjoy much success and the home side was dismissed for 33, the great man taking nine of their wickets at a personal cost of 20 runs.

The next year, the club moved to the Hough, where it was to remain for the best part of a century. Many exciting games were played there, but none compared with the Testimonial Match held on 26 April 1953, to celebrate the 80th birthday of the legendary Sydney Barnes. The sides which met that day — captained respectively by Bill Edrich and R.W.V. Robins (both of Middlesex and England) — included no less than nine county captains and 14 Test players, who thoroughly enjoyed themselves before 5,000 worshippers in a game which produced 529 runs, (Barnes XI, 240 (for 4 dec.), England XI, 289 (for 6)) Denis Compton contributing a quick 50 in even time, and Norman Yardley an even quicker one in 21 minutes, largely at the expense of Walter Robins, who conceded 53 runs in five overs. (To complete the picture, the umpires — Frank Chester and 'Tiger' Smith — were as distinguished in their own field as the players were in theirs.) R.W.V. (Walter) Robins was a contemporary of mine at Stafford Grammar School. A cricket and soccer Blue at Cambridge, he went on to captain Middlesex and make 19 Test appearances for England. Though he will chiefly be remembered as a cricketer, he was also a talented footballer: he played at outside right for Nottingham Forest, and was a regular member of the Corinthians when they could match the professionals, and competed in the FA Cup.

Though the town's most distinguished cricketer, Robins left Stafford while still in his early teens and never played for the town club. Of those who did, one of the most remarkable was 'Billy' Sheldon, a local tobacconist. The only one-armed cricketer I ever saw, he could drive the ball with tremendous power and scored thousands of runs for the club; but the most prolific run-scorer the club ever had was W.H. Twigg, the hockey international. In a game in 1906, he scored 206 not out, an extraordinary performance in a Saturday afternoon match. After the Second World War, Norman Browning, the town's Chief Education Officer and a regular opener for Bedfordshire before coming to Stafford, revived memories of the great days of Walter Twigg when he created a club record, scoring 527 runs in the month of August 1952.

League cricket was not played in Stafford until 1980, when the local club joined the North Staffs and South Cheshire League and created a record for that competition in its first season. In a game against Crewe, their professional, Peter Webb, and local batsman John McCredie, took part in a partnership of 179. Webb, a player of international class, scored 145 not out in that match; and cricket enthusiasts who watch televised games (and their name is legion) saw him open the New Zealand batting in the third of the one-day internationals against England this year (1984).

By the turn of the century, Stafford Hockey club was already well established as one of the strongest sides in the Midlands, with two internationals, W.H. Twigg and W.H.B. Bunn, in the team. (Walter Twigg must surely run Walter Robins close for the title of the finest allround sportsman the county town ever produced. Apart from his prowess as a hockey player, he was a regular member of the County Cricket XI, an outstanding billiards player and a crack shot!) Surprisingly, in view of its earlier record, the club was not revived after the 1914–18 war. For the next 15 years, local hockey players had to travel to Stone for a game and it was not until 1933 that the club was re-formed, with Walter

Twigg as Chairman. The game was again suspended on the outbreak of war in 1939, but this time there was no question about its revival: play was resumed at the Hough in 1946, and Walter Twigg lived to see its finest performance when it went through the 1955–56 season without defeat, and with the following remarkable record: played 23; won 22; drawn 1; lost 0; goals, 87, against 20.

The club added another international to its ranks when Robin Bailey, the current captain of Ireland, joined it after its record-breaking season, while Arthur Broadhurst (who had scored a large proportion of those 87 goals) had an international trial in the early sixties. A more competitive element was infused into local hockey when the club joined the Second Division of the Midland League in 1975; while its early seasons were undistinguished, it produced another international in John Moore, who played for the England under-19 side in 1980.

George Orwell's 1984 promised to be an historic year for the cricket and hockey clubs — or rather club, since they are now one entity. The rural scene at the Hough, with its surrounding gardens and allotments, had long since disappeared, leaving only an isolated green square, hemmed in by factory buildings. A move to less claustrophobic surroundings was inevitable, and with the assistance of the General Electric Company it came this year. On 2 April 1984 the club left the five acres at the Hough for 16½ acres at Riverway, where there are two cricket squares and five hockey pitches. The cricket club now have a professional, John Aldridge, the Worcestershire seam bowler, as captain; while the hockey club, with a host of young players, now fields six sides. The future, surely, is full of promise.

The soccer and rugby football clubs are reputed to have been founded in the same year, 1876, but the position is not free from doubt. That the soccer club was in existence then — or even earlier — is clear enough: an enquiry from 'Stranger' in *The Staffordshire Advertiser* on 30 September 1876, as to whether there was a football club in Stafford was answered in the next edition when its captain, Mr A. Cotton, assured him that there was, and 'play for the season will commence today at the Lammascotes'. The club referred to was Stafford Rangers, but the evidence regarding the existence of a separate rugby football club at the same time raises some intriguing questions, relying as it does on a report in an earlier edition of the same newspaper, of a match between Stafford and Newport on 26 February, which Stafford won by a goal and two tries to a goal. The reference to tries suggests a rugger match, but that could be misleading: the difference between the two codes was not so clearly defined then as it is now, and the description of the Stafford team, consisting of forwards, half backs and *two* backs, sounds like a soccer eleven. But the punch line comes at the end, when mention is made of a number of 'gentlemen worthy of notice in the Stafford team'. And the last name on that list of 'worthy gentlemen'? A. Cotton (Capt), no less. Which may well mean that the soccer and rugger clubs were not only founded in the same year, but were the same team with the same captain! A logical explanation could be that the original club was a soccer eleven which played an occasional game of rugger in a bastard form not uncommon at the time, some of whose members broke away after a few years to form a separate rugger club.

Stafford Rangers moved from the Lammascotes after a few years, first to Stone Road, then to a ground in Newtown (with a notorious brook, said to have been the resting place of more than one referee who had displeased the customers), before finally arriving at Marston Road in 1896, where they still play. It is not known when the rugger club left the Lammascotes, but by 1912 they were playing in Tixall Road. The Rangers turned professional in 1885 (3s 6d a game, with a 3s bonus for a draw and the princely sum of 5s 6d for a win), but their early years were undistinguished. After celebrating their Golden Jubilee in 1926–27 by winning the Birmingham League, they had to wait almost another 50 years before their greatest achievement; but it was worth waiting for. The late Roy Chapman, whose untimely death last year (1983) shocked the many friends he had made at Marston Road, was appointed manager in 1970, and within two years had transformed a struggling club into the best non-league side in the country. In their 1971–72 season, Rangers completed a memorable treble when they defeated Barnet in the Final of the FA Challenge Trophy at Wembley, before winning the championship of the Northern Premier League and the Staffordshire Senior Cup. Two years later, they were acclaimed in the national press as giantkillers, when they defeated three league sides on their way to the Fourth Round of the FA Cup before being beaten, 2–1, by Third Division Peterborough, in a nailbiting contest on Stoke City's ground, before a gate of 30,000.

The Rangers' decline began when Chapman left to manage Fourth Division Stockport in 1975. His successor Colin Meldrum's sojourn at Marston Road was as short as it was remarkable, when it looked as if the near miracle of the 1971–72 treble might be repeated, 'the Borough' falling at the last hurdle in all three competitions. The Northern Premier League was lost by a single point; in the FA Trophy Final, they were defeated 3–2 by Scarborough, in the dying seconds of extra time; the loss of the Staffs Senior Cup at the hands of a young Stoke City side was something of an anticlimax. Then came the first of a series of shocks when Meldrum ws sacked after a successful, if frustrating season, to become the first of seven managerial changes in as many years.

In the meantime, the rugger club had had its share of success and failure. It had suffered heavily when a number of its younger players lost their lives in the 1914–18 war, and it was not easy to get the club back on its feet when hostilities ended. A major problem was to find a ground. It was not until 1924 that they managed to obtain one in Rickerscote Road, where they remained for only two seasons before moving to Wolverhampton Road. Neither ground was satisfactory. In the first instance, a room at the Baths Inn served as the club house; in the second, the Vine provided the necessary accommodation. Since both these hostelries were in the centre of the town, the provision of transport to the ground remained a major problem. But difficulties are made to be overcome. Through the generosity of its President, Lord Stafford, the club was able to make its final move to its Newport Road ground after the Second World War, while its playing strength had been improved when King Edward VI School went over to rugger in

1935. One of the outstanding players it provided was D.G. Ashton, a schoolboy international who represented his country against Wales in 1949.

The club's greatest success came on Monday, 8 September 1963 when, against all the odds, it defeated by 6 points to 3, Old Roma, an Italian side containing nine internationals, which had been narrowly beaten, 16–14, by the Harlequins, at Twickenham, two days earlier. Subsequent progress has not been so dramatic, but satisfactory enough. While the amateur code has no league competition as such, it now has an equivalent in the Mercian Merit Table which the Stafford club won last year (1983), after being runners-up in the two previous seasons. In the meantime, the more elderly members have not been forgotten, and a XV of over-35s now engages other veterans in friendly combat. The club has gone so far as to install floodlights for training sessions to strengthen tired limbs and muscles.

The best known name to appear on the teamsheet was that of Andy Hancock, who captained the side in 1969–70, a name which had found its way into the record books in 1963, when he scored perhaps the most famous try ever to be seen at Twickenham, running the length of the field to equalise against Scotland in the dying seconds of a Calcutta Cup match. Mike Coulman, a local policeman, was another international who started his career with the Stafford club. After leaving Rising Brook School in 1962, he spent five years with them before joining Moseley, after which he made ten appearances for his country and toured South Africa with the British Lions.

Reg Berks followed Colin Meldrum as Stafford Rangers' manager in 1976, only to resign after one season. When Roy Chapman returned, hopes rose high and the Marston Roaders were delighted when their idol took his team on their third visit to Wembley, where they won the FA Trophy for the second time. Then the blow fell and the unbelievable happened. 'The Borough' made a poor start in the newly-formed Alliance Premier League and Chapman, by far their most successful manager, was sacked in January 1980. Thereafter, everything went disastrously wrong. Rangers finished second from bottom in 1980, and only escaped relegation because there was no team eligible for promotion; after two more poor seasons, the nadir was reached in May 1983, when they finished bottom, and their relegation to the Northern Premier League came almost as a relief. Hope of an immediate return to the Alliance were dashed when Rangers made an appalling start in the lower league, and when Colin Clarke, the latest of the string of managers, was sacked with the new season only a few weeks old, the punch-drunk Marston Roaders were angry and bewildered, with the great days of the Chapman era still fresh in their memory. Then along came Ron Reid and the picture changed, just as it had done when Roy Chapman took control in 1970. When Ron first occupied the hot seat in September 1983, Rangers were floundering at the bottom of the NP League; at the time of writing (March 1984), they have gone 15 league games without defeat, and there is good reason to hope that Ron will rejuvinate the club as effectively as Roy did more than a decade ago.

A hint of the darker side of sport had appeared in the advertisement of the first race meeting on the Common in 1820: 'A Main of Cocks will be fought during the

Races, between the Gentlemen of Staffordshire and Cheshire, for 5 guineas a battle and 200 the Main'. There had been a cockpit in Foregate since 1662, but it was not only cockfighting which defaced the sporting scene: bear- and bull-baiting were amongst the more barbarous sports of the time. Bears were bred specifically to serve in the pits, where they were tethered before being savaged by dogs, while bulls were tortured to the point of madness before being released to suffer a similar ordeal. There are horrific stories of dogs having to be cut away from the bleeding hide of a bull, with a sharp knife, when they refused to loosen their hold. Ratting matches were another popular diversion for so-called sportsmen, when a sackful of rats was emptied into a pit, to be torn to pieces by competing dogs: in 1823, Bill, a champion ratter, despatched 100 in five minutes. Bear-baiting had been outlawed by 1750 but, although bull-baiting was forbidden in Stafford in 1790, it was carried on clandestinely in the suburbs, well into the 1820s.

After bear- and bull-baiting had ceased, fights between the dogs themselves became popular, when they were matched, pound for pound, in organised contests, with a referee and timekeeper, and rules similar to those relating to the bare-knuckled pugilists of the day. Nothing was overlooked: even the untimely intervention of the law was provided for: 'In any case of Police interference, the Referee to name the next time and place for fighting'. In those rough days, the bull terrier was not normally kept as a pet but for what he could win as a fighting dog and, as a consequence, he acquired an undeserved reputation for ferocity and violence which persisted well into the present century. It was not until 1935 that he achieved respectability when recognised by the Kennel Club as a thoroughbred breed.

If we are to consider the Staffordshire bull terrier in the context of its county town, what better occasion to introduce it than the opening of the inn bearing its name? The Mayor, Councillor Harold Doffman, with other distinguished guests, attended the official opening of the Staffordshire Bull in May 1978, by a celebrity eminent in his field. Everything went according to plan and the manager, Graham Battens, did not complain when the visiting star, Brintiga of Shermor (known to his friends as Bruce) refused a pint of his best bitter and settled for a bowl of milk. An aristocrat of his kind, Bruce behaved impeccably throughout the opening ceremony, and the photograph of a fearsome hound, baring a terrifying set of teeth and with an apprehensive manager on the end of his leash, does him less than justice. Another dog had chosen to trespass across the photographer's line of vision just as he was about to press the button, and Bruce didn't like it. Bruce was a Staffordshire bull terrier with an impressive pedigree, but like those of his human counterparts his ancestors must have been a mixed bag. If we could trace our ancestry back far enough, most of us would find a few villains hanging on the family tree, and no doubt Bruce had the occasional bull-baiter to blot the family escutcheon. Abraham Fleming might well have been referring to one of them when, in *Old English Dogges* (c1570), he described one of his 'dogges' as '. . . huge . . . burthensome of body . . . Terrible and Fearfulle to behold'. This is believed to have been an Old

English Mastiff, from which the Staffordshire bull terrier evolved when the bulldog was crossed with the terrier.

The popularity of the breed in the county town is due to the efforts of local pioneers like Bruce's owners, Morris and Shirley Simpson, whose thoroughbred pups have been sold into various parts of the country. Bruce (or should we call him Brintiga?) was no ordinary dog: he had a mind of his own. This business of dog shows, for instance. He was prepared to attend them, but only with an escort of his choice: honours were there for the taking, but he would only compete for them if accompanied by the Simpsons' 13-year-old daughter, Dawn. When she joined the WRNS in 1979, Bruce took it as a personal affront and retired from active competition.

The Simpsons founded the Stafford SBT Owners Club in time for their dogs (including two of Bruce's sons) to attend the first birthday party of the Staffordshire Bull, an event which, said the press, 'proved a howling success'. Let Shirley Simpson have the last word about the breed she loves: 'They are', she says, 'small and compact, adjust well to any reasonable living conditions and are wonderful friends and companions, very loyal and, above all, perfect gentlemen and ladies'. What more is there left to say?

Stafford Cycling Club (1880). (SCCM)

ABOVE: The galaxy of cricket stars (with officials) who took part in Sydney Barnes Testimonial Match, at the Hough, 26 April 1953: (L to R) back: J. Young (Middlex), C. Palmer (Leics), L. Goodwin (Leics), D. Haynes (Staffs), N. E. Hollies (Warwicks), R.V.C. Robins; middle: T. Muir (Scorer), T.H. Higson (Stafford CC), E. Smith (Umpire), N.E. Browning (Beds & Staffs), J.D. Robertson (Middlex), P.H.S. Wadham (Stafford), R.T.D. Perks (Worcs), C.W.Grove (Warwicks), W.S. Surridge (Surrey), J.T. Ikin (Lancs), C. Goodway (Warwicks), R.T. Spooner (Warwicks), F. Chester (Umpire), C.H. Green (Scorer); front: R.T. Simpson (Notts), C. Washbrook (Lancs), W.J. Edrich (Middlex), S.F. Barnes, J.T.W. Neville (Stafford CC President), R.W.V. Robins (Middlex), N.W.D. Yardley (Yorks), D.C.S. Compton (Middlex), K. Dollery (Warwicks). (SCC) BELOW: Stafford Cricket Club President's Day, 1980: standing: J. Boucher, A. Dobson, N. Williams, D. Hallett, D. Talbot, R. Churchill, (— Scorer); seated: B. Williams, J. McCredie, A. M. Bulpitt, K. Williams, D. Duxbury. (SCC)

ABOVE: Visit of Bangladesh National side to play Stafford Cricket Club at the Hough, 1982. (SCC) BELOW: Stafford Hockey Club. 'The Vets', 1980: David Moore, John Moore, John Barker, Dennis Wall, David Barker, Colin Sproston, John Milner, Alan Machin, Gordon McMullan, Eddie Bowers, Danny Doyle. (SHC) INSET: Chairman Walter Twigg, the talented amateur: hockey international, county cricketer, et al. (SHC)

51

Walter Robins, as a 13-year-old schoolboy, in the Grammar School soccer and cricket First XIs.
OPPOSITE ABOVE: Stafford Grammar School Soccer XI, 1918–19: From L to R back: E.
Ward, J.R. Bithell, T. Blake, — Mawdsley; middle: J. Day, W. Somers, W. Wisdom (Capt), F.
Page, T.H. Tufft,; front: R.W.V. Robins, R. Jones. BELOW: Stafford Grammar School Cricket
XI, 1919: Walter Robins is seated, fourth from the left, with Frank Page (Capt) on his right.
Walter's brother, Vernon Robins, is in the front row (right). ABOVE: Stafford Rangers, 1971–72,
winners of Northern Premier League Championship, FA Trophy and Staffordshire Senior Cup.
('SN') BELOW: Manager Roy Chapman leading out his team at Wembley, 15 April 1972. ('E&S')

OPPOSITE ABOVE: Captain Graham Chadwick receiving the FA Trophy from Sir Stanley Rouse and BELOW: the welcome home. (Both 'E&S') ABOVE: The same team, still fighting fit 11 years later, when they defeated an All-Stars XI at Marston Road, 1 May 1983. ('SN') BELOW: Stafford Rugby Union FC, 1931–32, back: R.S. Dunstan, C.M. Averill, J.H.N. Lander, R.J.C. Evans, J.E. Coates, H.R. Moulton, T. Rees, H.A. Johnston; seated: G. Sandham, E. Robertson, W.N.J. Somers (Capt), W.E. Streete (President), P.T. Davies, G.H. Bostock, R.H.P Barter; front: G.N. Gossling, A.J. Evans, F.H. Stokes, L.G. Wilson. (SRUFC)

ABOVE: Stafford Rugby Union FC 1945–46: back: H. Wilson (Capt), A. I. James, J.H. Farmer, R.J. Collier, T.R. Hollins, D. Parrott, B.J. Stewart, L. Banks; front: P.K. Brodie, R.B. White, J.McColl, G. Longdon, G.C. Selwin, J. Collier, A.W.C. Webb. (SRUFC) BELOW: The Royal Brine Baths and boathouse and OPPOSITE ABOVE: the interior (Swimming Gala in 1920s), where water polo was played until 1950. This sport was popular between the wars, when the local side enjoyed considerable success, winning the North Staffs Water Polo League in 1924 and 1930, and the Staffordshire Water Polo Cup in 1930 and 1937. (SCCM)

LEFT: The Staffordshire Bull Inn, (TB) opened by local celebrity RIGHT: Brintiga of Shermor ('Bruce') in May 1978. (SS)

ABOVE: Corporation Street, the first Board School opened at Stafford in 1895. BELOW: Corporation Street School staff (1905).

LESSONS LEARNT

It was not until the Factory Acts were making their first futile attempts to restrain the exploitation of children that the State accepted any responsibility for their education. Until then, it had been content to leave it in the hands of the church, and associated organisations. The first Sunday School was opened by the Wesleyans in 1805; the first day-school, St Austin's, by the Roman Catholics, in Wolverhampton Road in 1818; the Methodists opened the British School in St Chad's Lane, in 1834; and St Mary's Church of England School was built on the site of the parish workhouse, to the south of the churchyard, in 1856. Churches and charities did excellent work but faced ever-increasing financial problems, but it was not until 1833 that the government stirred itself: grants were then made for the building of schools, Board Schools were established in 1870 and compulsory school attendance was introduced for the first time. A National School was opened in Rowley Street in 1874, but 21 years were to pass before the first Board School appeared in Corporation Street, and classes for pupil teachers were started there in 1898.

The private establishments which had helped to fill the gap varied from those taught by a qualified teacher (usually a clergyman) to the so-called Dame School. There was a Boarding School for Young Ladies in the Market Square in the 1760s, and a section of the High House was being used as a Ladies' Academy at about the same time. Of the later private establishments, one of the best was opened in 1820 by the Congregational Minister, Rev John Chalmers, in premises adjoining his Zion Chapel in Martin Street, before moving into Eastgate the next year. Described as a Commercial and Classical Academy, it was of a high standard in the context of the day. As a small boy, I attended one of the private schools which survived into the present century. Sackvilles, in Eastgate Street, was typical of the better type of Dame School, the staff comprising the elderly Mrs Sackville and her spinster daughter, Ethel. Apart from reading and writing, we did not learn much, except good manners and respect for our elders, subjects which could be taught, with advantage, at some of the more pretentious establishments of today. Eastgate Street has changed a lot since I started my schooldays there during the First World War, but the little house where the Sackvilles had their school is still there, looking much the same (though somehow much smaller) as it did when I first climbed the stone steps to its front door, a packet of sandwiches clutched in my sticky little paw.

Stafford now has two independent schools, each far removed from the modest little private affairs of the past. Brooklands was founded two years after the passing of the Education Act 1944, by a number of parents prepared to pay for the privilege of sending their children to the school of their choice. Opened in Eccleshall Road in September 1946, with a tiny group of five and six-year-olds, it made remarkable progress. Adjoining premises were purchased in 1962 and a new assembly hall built, linking the junior and senior departments, while science laboratories were added five years later. With Mr D.A. Ashton, MA, Dip Ed at its head, it now has 170 pupils to the age of 13, and a curriculum which includes all the subjects required for scholarships and entrance examinations to the public schools, a fitting tribute to those pioneers who made it all possible 40 years ago. Stafford Independent Grammar School is only two years old and the first few years are bound to be difficult; but with its experienced and enthusiastic headmaster, Dr J.R. Garrood, MA, PhD, there is no reason why it should not enjoy the same success at Burton Manor as Brooklands has in Eccleshall Road. This second independent school complements the first: students are prepared for GCE and CSE 'O' Levels and, in the sixth form, 'A' Levels and Oxbridge entry. Brooklands School should provide a healthy proportion of its annual intake; if all goes well, they will together fly the flag of independence for many years to come.

Though the development of elementary education was so slow and laboured, there had been a Grammar School in the town from time immemorial. Edward VI is credited with having founded it in 1550, but such a school, attached to the Collegiate Church of St Mary, had been in existence, in some form or other, for centuries: it would be more accurate to say that Edward re-founded it when it was saved from the wreck in which most of the others foundered on the dissolution of the monasteries. It was to enjoy a chequered career. When it moved to Gaol Square in 1801, after some 200 years at St Bertelin's Chapel, there were 120 boys on the register. Forty years later there were 14, after Rev Joseph Shaw, one of its best headmasters, had been followed by Rev George Norman, one of its worst.

The school moved to its final home in Newport Road in 1862. Norman's immediate successors were an indifferent trio, but the Governors stopped the rot when they appointed Rev H.J. Ferrier, MA, in 1877. Though shackled by lack of funds, the school prospered under his leadership, a Preparatory Department was opened at the bottom, and a sixth form at the top. Ferrier also built the wall along Friars Road, at his own expense. The seeds he sowed bore fruit. When he resigned in 1884, the number of pupils had more than doubled and he was followed by the first layman to be appointed.

A.E. Laing, MA, was a distinguished mathematician, whose text books were widely used by secondary schools. While this did little to endear him to the boys, cricket was a different matter, and his stock rose high when he drove a ball over the school building and into the brook in Newport Road. In 17 years (1884–1901) he achieved much, providing what he described as 'a course of education sufficiently wide to give any boy the education he may require, whether Classical or the so-called Commercial'. Laing's career ended on a tragic note when his wife died, bursting a blood vessel after a fit of coughing, a personal calamity which affected his mental balance. Within a year of her death, he retired and gave way to E.O. Powell, BA, probably the best known and most respected headmaster of them all.

I made my unobtrusive appearance on the scene in 1916 and, during the decade I spent at the school, I was privileged to see both Mr Powell and his much maligned successor, Mr Nott, at close quarters. A classical scholar, courteous and dignified, some sort of mystique seemed to surround 'Johnny' Powell, and to many of his pupils — especially in retrospect — he represented near-perfection. A lone Philistine, I was never able to understand the Powell legend which grew stronger as his era faded further into the past: there must have been some magic about him which escaped me, perhaps because I only knew him in the twilight of his career. The school enjoyed considerable academic success during 'Johnny's' reign, but in his later years he was a sick man, the school suffered as a consequence and discipline became slack. When he retired in 1924, a disciplinarian was sorely needed, and that was what the school got when F.T. Nott was appointed to succeed him. It would be difficult to imagine anyone so utterly different, in every respect, from Powell. A short, irascible little man, he did not suffer fools gladly; he could be frank to the point of rudeness, and with his uncompromising approach was never a popular man. In his first few difficult years, he lived in the shadow of E.O. Powell, and few would have dared suggest that he would do as much for the school as his predecessor. I am one of those few who believe that he did more. He was too impatient to be a good teacher, but he was a first class administrator and the architect of a school which improved beyond recognition while he was at the helm.

By no means all his innovations met with general approval. The change from soccer to rugger and the consquent demise of the Old Edwardians AFC was resented by some Old Boys, and the introduction of the prefect system was just as unpopular at first. But the Head knew what he was doing and it was soon working remarkably well. I remember the first prefects' meeting, when he emphasised the important role we had to play in what amounted virtually to a crusade. The first of our breed, we had approached our responsibilities uneasily, but our confidence grew as we were persuaded that the school might collapse in ruins and Mr Nott's own career come to an untimely end, if we failed in our duty.

One of those duties was to read the lesson at morning prayers, and a near disaster will remain etched in my memory for ever. It was the Head's practice to enter in his diary the lesson to be read the next morning, and I usually consulted it the evening before. By the grace of God, I did so on this occasion, and when I showed it to F.T.N. and suggested that it was just possible that he had made a mistake, he readily admitted that he had and thanked me for saving us both from what he described as a temporary embarrassment. That was the understatement of the year: The Lesson Which Was Never Read came from the Old Testament, and referred (*inter alia*, as the lawyers say) to Onan. *Res ipsa loquitur* (as they also say.)

My departure at Christmas, 1926, was only one of the improvements the school was to enjoy under F.T. Nott: within the next few years, its face had completely changed. Major building extensions were opened by the Lord Lieutenant of the county, Lord Harrowby, in December 1928, and four years later Nott was elected to the Headmasters' Conference and King Edward VI, Stafford, became a public school.

On the outbreak of war, though he would have been better advised to remain at the school, Major F.T. Nott insisted on resuming his military career, and Mr J.

Poole was appointed Acting Headmaster. A quiet man, with a rich sense of humour, 'Jim' Poole faced many problems, including loss of staff and the arrival of Chatham House to an already overcrowded school, on their evacuation from Ramsgate in June 1940. The value of his contribution during the war years was inestimable and, when a sick Mr Nott returned in 1945, 'Jim' had established himself as a much respected headmaster. Nott had suffered a crippling stroke while serving in Iraq, it was distressingly obvious that he was incapable of resuming his duties and he retired in February 1946. F.T. Nott, MA (Oxon) had many critics but, when he died on 30 April 1950, the school lost an outstanding headmaster.

D.J.D. Smith MA (1946–1960) and L. Bampton, MA (1961–1976) came upon the scene at a time of revolutionary change. The Education Act 1944, purporting to offer 'equal opportunity for all', was beginning to take effect, the differences between Elementary and Grammar schools were swept away, Primary and Secondary took their place and the much-criticised 11-plus examination was introduced to decide, at that tender age, for which type of education a child was best fitted. The 11-plus completely changed the structure and character of schools like King Edward VI. By the early 1950s, the number of boys had virtually doubled and the curriculum had to be expanded to meet their needs but, in spite of the difficulties which Smith and his staff had to face, the school enjoyed considerable success, both academically and in the field of sport. Bampton's problems were different but just as daunting. The introduction of comprehensive education had been a lengthy and complicated business, and a number of economic crises had delayed the provision of the new schools to house the various 'streams' of pupils at different levels. It was not until 1976 that the reorganisation into primary, middle and high schools was finally completed; and when the boys' Grammar School and the girls' High School together became King Edward VI High School, Bampton's services were recognised when he was appointed Headmaster of the new establishment.

When E.O. Powell took up his appointment at the Grammar School in 1901, there had been no similar establishment available for girls. When he retired in 1924, there were 250 boys at his school while the girls' High School, at the Oval in Lichfield Road, had 350 children on its roll; surely a complete answer to those who had considered it a waste of time and money to provide secondary education for girls. When a school for girls was opened at Moat House in 1903, the newly-created Education Authority regarded it with suspicion, if not actual disapproval. Four years later, when the number of girls had trebled from 40 to 120, it bowed to public opinion, purchased a plot of land in Lichfield Road and opened the Girls' High School in September, 1907. Spared the staff difficulties which had beset the Grammar School in its early years, much of its subsequent success stemmed from the quality of its headmistresses, the last three — Miss G.J. 'Ma' McCrea (1910–1937), Miss L. Whitehurst (1937–1959) and Miss C.N. Dawson (1959–1976) spanning a period of 66 years.

'Ma' McCrea had much in common with E.O. Powell. For 14 years their careers ran alongside; and though Miss McCrea was never quite the legendary figure which Powell became after his retirement, her school developed more rapidly than his and provided better facilities for boarders. There were never more than a handful at Newport Road, but there were so many at the Oval that the school buildings could not accommodate them. In 1909, they moved to Hough Cottage, Lichfield Road, where — to quote Miss Kathleen Payne-Hall, one of the original boarders — 'a very happy household' produced a play at the end of the summer term and held an annual Fancy Dress Ball to which the staff, '[who] wore skirts which touched the ground', were invited.

The school enjoyed much academic success under Miss McCrea, but one of its shortcomings was the accent it placed on the training of pupils for the teaching profession, to the exclusion of everything else. Frustrating though this must have been for a girl with wider ambitions, it reflected public opinion in the twenties, when the 'career woman' was regarded as something of a freak. During the Whitehurst and Dawson eras all that was changed, and the ladies began their successful invasion of most of the professions. And so the school prospered, and perhaps the most significant part of one of Miss Dawson's later reports was that only six girls had applied for teacher training.

The founders of Moat House had not been the only pioneers in the field: opposite the new High School in Lichfield Road, a similar establishment was enjoying equal success. St Joseph's Convent School owed its existence to the devotion of a few French nuns, driven from their homeland by secularisation laws which made it impossible for them to carry on their chosen vocation. Four of them arrived in England in 1903, to be followed the next year by three others, including Mère Jeanne, their first Mother Superior, a remarkable woman who played an outstanding part, not only in the religious life of the Order, but in the founding and development of a convent school which was to form an important part of the educational and cultural life of the town. Responsible for the building extensions of 1923 and '32 which the growth of the school demanded, she was spared long enough to see all her plans come to fruition and, when she died in the mid-thirties, the premises in Lichfield Road not only housed a Convent for the Sisters but a flourishing Girls' School as well. By 1950, there were 360 girls on the roll, 45 of them boarders.

Accommodation problems at the boys' school had been eased when a second Grammar School, the Graham Balfour, was opened in Stone Road by the County Council in 1962. Six years later, it was absorbed into the new educational system, when it became the upper school of the Trinity Fields Comprehensive, which was renamed Graham Balfour High School in 1973. The merits and demerits of comprehensive education have been and, no doubt, will continue to be the subject of endless debate. Wherever the truth lies, the local educational scene is impressive: as well as its quota of primary, middle and high schools and its two independent establishments, further education is available at the College in Earl Street and the North Staffs Polytechnic at Beaconside.

When the Boys' Grammar and the Girls' High Schools merged to become King Edward VI High School, each lost it separate identity but survived as a school, albeit of a different kind. St Joseph's Convent suffered a harsher fate. When the

Blessed William Howard became the Catholic comprehensive school for Stafford and district, the Convent's raison d'être came to an end and, with it, the school itself. It had always been self-supporting and, when it closed its doors in 1971, they closed for ever. But although the school has gone, Mère Jeanne's Convent still remains as a religious house, a refuge for the sick and needy, who are never turned away from its doors. There are some things which even comprehensive education cannot destroy.

ABOVE: St Mary's Church of England School. (KEHS) BELOW: Pupils at drill in the yard of Rowley Street National School (c1906).

ABOVE: Miss Laing's Private School group (c1895). There were 18 private schools in Stafford in 1863, ten of which survived into the present century. (SCCM) LEFT: The premises in Eastgate Street which once housed Sackville's Private School, almost unchanged since the author started his schooldays there during the First World War. RIGHT: The Congregational Zion Chapel, Martin Street, whose Minister, Rev John Chalmers, founded a Commercial and Classical Academy adjoining the Chapel, in 1820. (SCCM)

65

ABOVE: Brooklands School, Eccleshall Road, founded after the passing of the Education Act, 1944. (BSch) BELOW: Brooklands School group, 1947. The school now has 170 pupils. (B Sch)

66

ABOVE; Stafford Independent Grammar School, Burton Manor, opened in 1982, and CENTRE: a physics class, with Headmaster, Dr Garrood. (Both SIGS) BELOW: The Collegiate Church of St Mary, to which a school was attached, probably as early as the XIIth century, from which the Grammar School evolved. (WSL)

ABOVE: St Bertelin's Chapel (adjoining St Mary's Church), where the Grammar School spent some 200 years before moving to Gaol Square in 1801. BELOW: The school in North Walls (c1837). (Both WSL)

ABOVE: The school in Newport Road, to which it moved in 1862. BELOW: King Edward VI School staff, 1924, when E.O. Powell (Headmaster, 1901–1924) retired, to be followed by F.T. Nott: (L to R) back: R. White, A. Field, C.A. Woodger, S.W. Arrowsmith; front: Mr Pritchard, N.B. Ker, R.C. Lambert, E.O. Powell, —, T.C. Howard, G.R. Fisher.

69

LEFT: F.T. Nott MA Headmaster, 1924–1946 (excluding the war years). (KEHS) RIGHT: The school, floodlit, to celebrate its fourth centenary (1950). BELOW: School Soccer XI, 1925–26: (L to R) Back: C.S. Kelly, L. Hunter, R.W. Riseley, H. Hammersley; middle: D.H. Jackson, D.W.T. Poole, E.C. MacDonald (Capt), S.W. Wade, G. Taylor; front: A.C. Balmforth, P.T.W. Butters. (KEHS)

ABOVE: Soccer XI, 1926–27: From L to R, back: J.L. Evans, R.W. Risely, C.M. Averill, K.C. Wood; middle: W.E. Lloyd, G. Boon, S.W. Wade (capt), P.T.W. Butters, A.C. Balmforth; front: A.C. MacDonald, D.A. Ebdon. (KEHS) Over the two seasons 1925–27, the Grammar School soccer side was beaten by only three schools – Wolverhampton, Newcastle and Newport –defeats were avenged in return fixtures. Of the remaining 23 games against other schools, 20 were won and 3 drawn, with a goal difference of 135 against 35. The 1925–26 team, with centre half Eric MacDonald as captain, was one of the best – arguably, perhaps the best *– the school ever fielded. LEFT: Moat House, Newport Road, where the Girls High School was born in 1903, and RIGHT: Miss E. Carless, Headmistress, 1903–1907. (KEHS)*

71

HOUGH COTTAGE, STAFFORD.

Licensed by the Governors of the Stafford Girls' High School as a Hostel for Girls from a distance who wish to attend the High School as either Terminal or Weekly Boarders.

Five Dormitories, Large Dining and School Rooms set apart for the use of the girls, and every care is taken that they shall enjoy the freedom and comforts of home. The Hostel, 3 minutes' walk from the High School, is delightfully situated, with Tennis Court, large Garden and Paddock.

Application may be made to the **Head of the Hostel, Miss M. G. JOHNSON,** or to the **Headmistress of the High School, Stafford.**

ABOVE: Stafford Girls High School, the Oval, Lichfield Road. BELOW: Hough Cottage, where the High School boarders – 'a very happy household' – were first accommodated in 1909.

LEFT: Miss M.E. de R. Phillp. Headmistress, High School 1907–1909. (KEHS) BELOW: High School hockey XI, 1913–14: (L to R) back: Violet Jackson, Hilda Hulme, Edna Pye, Miss Milton, Charlotte Simms, Grace Wright; middle: Mary Tildesley, Winifred Lloyd (Capt), Miss G.J. McCrea (headmistress), Eileen Arrowsmith, Nellie Hurlstone; front: Kathleen Chadderton, — (KEHS) RIGHT: Miss L. Whitehurst, Headmistress, 1937–1959. (KEHS)

ABOVE: St Joseph's Convent, the other girls' school in Lichfield Road, founded in 1903 by four French nuns and Mère Jeanne, their first Mother Superior. (SJ's C) BElOW: The grounds of the convent.

ABOVE: The Borough Library, 1914. LEFT: The William Salt Library, treasurehouse of local history, in Market Square, 1913, and RIGHT: in its present premises in Eastgate Street. (Both WSL)

ABOVE: The Elizabethan Town Hall in Market Square, the first floor of which was used as a theatre in the 18th century. (WSL) BELOW: The Borough Hall.

STAGE AND SCREEN

The story of the local theatre is one of a continuous struggle for survival, a surprising state of affairs in a town with a long theatrical tradition. Stafford had been a regular port of call for the strolling players of the 17th century, and there is evidence to suggest that Shakespeare himself visited the county town in 1610. The appearance of the King's Players in that year is recorded in the Stafford Borough Account Book; and since it was their last provincial tour before the retirement of their most famous member to New Place, Stratford, there must surely be a strong probability that he accompanied them. The first permanent theatre of which there are existing records was the Elizabethan Town Hall, the first floor of which was used for that purpose for more than 50 years, until its demolition in the 1790s. Playbills of the time can be seen at the William Salt Library, on which the name of Stanton first appears, a remarkable theatrical family which provided, not only the manager but many of the actors, for the best part of a century. It was Samuel Stanton who built the theatre in Martin Street (later to be called the Lyceum) in 1792, and he and his family were responsible for the appearance of a number of distinguished London actors at an obscure little provincial theatre, whose visits helped to keep it alive.

When the last of the Stantons took his final bow in 1838, the theatre 'went dark' for a decade, and although it managed to eke out a bare existence for another 77 years — punctuated by frequent periods of 'darkness' — it was a blow from which it never really recovered. By 1852, Dickens was calling it 'a mouldy little theatre', and thereafter it continued a gradual decline until it fell into such a state of disrepair that the Corporation refused to renew its lease in 1912. Even then, it refused to accept defeat; extensive repairs were carried out and, within six months, it had reopened as the Playhouse. However the end was near — only three uncertain years remained, before it was gutted by fire on the night of 4 June 1915.

The only serious attempt to replace the Playhouse was a disastrous failure. Described in the press as 'a magnificent building . . . erected in Sandon Road . . . for the complete staging of the most modern plays. . .', the Sandonia opened in November 1920, with the record-breaking musical, *Chu Chin Chow* but, although the novelty of a new theatre kept it alive for a time, it was doomed to failure from the first. Built at the north end of the town while most of its playgoers came from the south, another fundamental mistake was made when the proprietors embarked on the impossible task of alternating a stage play one week with a film the next. As a result, the Sandonia 'died the death' as a theatre, within only a few years, to survive as a second-rate cinema until the mid-sixties, when it ended its days as a bingo hall.

For the next 60 years, the county town was without a theatre. The Borough Hall provided facilities of a kind for theatrical productions — usually by frustrated amateur societies who deserved something better — but it never pretended to be a theatre, in any sense of the word. Such cultural activities were only incidental to its main function as an office, housing the local government departments. Then, in the late 1970s, local government moved to the Riverside Civic Offices and major alterations were carried out on the Borough Hall. While its outer shell remained unaltered, its interior was completely transformed and Stafford suddenly found itself not with one theatre but two, together with facilities for other social and cultural activities.

The new project was expensive, to say the least, but the result was impressive, embracing not only the theatres and rehearsal rooms, but a public bar and restaurant (the Globe Tavern), and two banqueting halls (the Mountbatten Suite and the Churchill Room) to accommodate 150 diners. The Gatehouse Theatre, with a separate entrance at the Market Street end of the building, is a model of modern design, with 570 seats which can be adjusted to provide a conventional proscenium theatre or a theatre in the round, and can — indeed, already does — cater for entertainments as diverse as a symphony concert and a snooker match. An up-to-date system of stage lighting is operated from a control room at the rear of the auditorium, and visiting companies find at their disposal a suite of dressing rooms, complete with showers, which compare favourably with those of a West End theatre. The more modest Cabin, a studio theatre with a film projector and screen, seats 120: it has served as a recording studio and can be used for a multitude of other purposes, from a jazz club to chamber music recitals.

The facilities provided by the new theatres attracted to the town professional entertainers of a high standard; but there remained a minority which enjoyed a 'straight' play or musical, which were not available. The Gatehouse and the Cabin supplied what was demanded; as time went by, the one- and two-night stands of 'pop' entertainers were leavened by weekly visits of touring companies with plays like *The Hollow, Lady Chatterley's Lover, Under Milk Wood, Hamlet,* and *Present Laughter.*

Unlike the theatre lover, the cinemagoer has always been well catered for since the Picture Palace first opened its doors more than 70 years ago, one at the front to the threepennies, the other at the back for the more expensive seats at sixpence and ninepence a time. (For the childrens' Saturday matinee, the noisiest and most exciting performance of the week, the prices were more reasonable — a penny at the front and threepence at the back.) When reporting the opening in July 1910, the press was more cautious in its use of adjectives than it was to be when the Sandonia came on the scene 10 years later. This was not a 'magnificent' building but a 'commodious' one and, while denied the luxuries of the theatre, it was 'comfortably fitted up', with 'a sloping floor which will enable every member of the audience to obtain a good view of the pictures'. In fact, it was a draughty, ramshackle wooden building, approached across a piece of waste land in Glover Street, but who cared? For a modest charge, you could see William S. Hart, one of the first of the cowboys, firing from the hip, and lovely, dewey-eyed Pearl White bound hand and foot to the railway line or facing a beetle-browed, heavily moustached villain, and a Fate Worse Than Death. When the Albert Hall opened its wrought iron gates in Crabbery Street in May 1912, it offered much the same fare, for the same prices, and the two cinemas ran alongside each other, quite happily, for another couple of years.

78

Their monopoly came to an end when Goodall's Pictures Ltd opened a third, shortly before the outbreak of the First World War. The Picture House was in a different category. Built in the main street, on the south side of the river bridge, its 'Old English' frontage and ornamental verandah fitted neatly into a pleasant area of the town, familiar to Staffordians and visitors alike, with the Brine Baths and its clock tower, and the Green Bridge boathouse on the other side of the river. Now all that has changed — all, that is, but the Picture House, which looks exactly the same as it did 70 years ago. Even the interior has hardly changed, the only apparent difference being the removal of the brass rail and curtain which used to divide the stalls from the balcony. As a regular patron of its early days, I can remember when a violinist, perched aloft in a tiny Romeo and Juliet balcony, provided soft music while tea and biscuits were served free, at the Wednesday and Saturday matinees. All very pleasant and genteel, and also providing more sophisticated entertainment, with admission fees (threepence to a shilling) little more than those charged in Glover and Crabbery Streets.

Sadly, the Picture Palace closed in 1923, its epitah a board advertising Ethel Clayton in *Enchantment*, which remained for months outside the deserted building; but after the Odeon was opened by the Earl of Shrewsbury in 1936, Stafford had four cinemas until the Albert Hall finally gave up the ghost in 1952, to be followed by the Sandonia a decade later. Today, the town again has four, three of them under the same roof, since the Astra Film Centre took over the Odeon in 1981, the fourth being the indestructible Picture House.

But for those of us who were young in the first decades of the century, nothing will ever match the excitement of the old Picture Palace and the incomparable Pearl White in *The Perils of Pauline* (To Be Continued.) You had to wait a week to find out whether she had been decapitated by the 3.15 from Paddington or crushed to death while stealing the Buddha's Eye. She never was, of course.

Lyceum Theatre advertisement, 1898, Victoria Road; Harry Thompson on the left.

The Last Night of the Company's performing in Town this Season,

For the Benefit of Mr. and Mrs. PALMER,

At the *Town-Hall* in *Stafford*,
On Friday Evening, the 27th of March, will be presented
A TRAGEDY, called

OTHELLO:

Moor of Venice,

(Written by Shakespear,)
BRABANTIO, by Mr. PALMER,
LODOVICO, by Mr. FREEMAN,
OTHELLO, by Mr. WALKER,
CASSIO, by Mr. FRYER,
IAGO, by Mr. STANTON,
RODORIGO, by Mr. COOPER,
DESDEMONA, by Mrs. COOPER,
ÆMILIA, by Mrs. BLANCHARD.

End of the 2nd Act, Mr. Palmer, will Read, a Periodical Whimsical Essay,
ON THE,

NEWS PAPERS,

In which will be introduc'd an

IRISH PETITION,

And a Letter from Mr.
Phœlimoguissnocarrclarneycavataughcadoganmacfrarne,
To his Daughter in London,
Between the Play and Farce, will be introduc'd a favourite Scene taken out of
Mr. FOOTE's Comedy of The

MINOR,

Mrs. COLE, by Mr. COOPER,
Sir GEORGE, by Mr. FRYER,
LOADER, by Mr. STANTON,
DICK, by Master STANTON,

With the following Entertainments of Dancing between the Acts, by Mr. Jackson, and Others.

Particularly The

Drunken PEASANT,

And the Jovial Shoe-Makers,

To which will be added a Farce call'd

The LYING VALET,

HARP, (the Lute or Viol) by Mr. PALMER,
FRY, by Mrs. BLANCHARD,

[illegible] Mr. Taylor's Bookseller, of Mr. Palmer at Mr.
[illegible], near the Market-Place.

On WEDNESDAY, December 27th, 1786, will be performed
A CONCERT of MUSIC.
BOXES 2s. 6d. PIT, 2s. GALLERY, 1s. To begin precisely at 6 o'Clock.

Between the several Parts of the Concert, will be presented (gratis) by his Majesty's Servants a Dramatic ROMANCE, (written by Garrick) called

CYMON,

Or, No Magic like Love.

With the original Overture, Airs, Duets, Chorusses, &c. New Machinery, Dresses, and Decorations.

The merry Linco,   Mr. OSBORNE,
Merlin, (an Enchanter,)   Mr. NEWPORT,
Justice Dorus,   Mr. COOPER,
Demon of Revenge,   Mr. JACKSON,
Principal Dancing Devil,   Mr. GARLAND,
Devils, Mr. PHILLIPS, Mr. BALY, and Mr. HARGRAVE,
And Cymon,   Mr. STOTT,
Fatima,   Mrs. FOX,
Urganda, (an Enchantress)   Mrs. MORRIS,
Cupid,   Miss JACKMAN,
Dorcas,   Mrs. COOPER,
And Sylvia,   Mrs. SAUNDERS.

In Act 1st, a Dance of Cupids, and the Loves, by the

CHILDREN of the TOWN,

In Act 4th,

A DANCE of DEVILS.

In Act 5th, a NEW SCENE of

The BLACK TOWER,

Which changes to a

TRIUMPHAL ARCH.

To which will be added, a FARCE called

MISS in her TEENS,

Or, a Medley of Lovers.

Captain Flash,   Mr. GARLAND,
Captain Loveit,   Mr. PHILLIPS,
Puff,   Mr. COOPER,
Jasper,   Mr. JACKSON,
And Fribble,   Mr. OSBORNE.
Tag,   Mrs. COOPER,
And Miss Biddy,   Mrs. SAUNDERS.

TICKETS for the Concert to be had at the Swan, Star, and Bear's Head Inns, at [illegible] New-Drovers, and of Mr. Osborne, at Mr. Heath's, next the Bridge, where Places for the BOXES may be taken.

To-morrow Evening for the last Time, the CASTLE of ANDALUSIA, the Songs, Airs, &c. may be had at the Theatre, and of Mrs. Boden and Son, Price 2d.

STAFFORD, Printed by S. BODEN and SON.

LEFT: *The year of this production of* Othello *at the Town Hall Theatre does not appear on the playbill, but it was probably in the 1770s. (WSL)* RIGHT: *The New Theatre was ill-named. Within a year of this production of* Cymon *in 1786, part of the building collapsed, and Stafford was without a theatre until Samuel Stanton built the one in Martin Street six years later. (WSL) OPPOSITE: It was after seeing her performance in this production of* The Wonder *that Sheridan took Harriot Mellon (the future Duchess of St Albans) from Martin Street to Drury Lane, where she made her London debut as Lydia Languish in his play,* The Rivals. *(WSL)*

By DESIRE of
R. B. Sheridan, Efq.

THEATRE STAFFORD,

This Present FRIDAY October the 24th

Will be Presented a Favourite COMEDY, call'd

The WONDER:

A Woman keeps a Secret!

Don Felix Mr. RUBERY

Don Lopez Mr. FORESTER—Don Pedro Mr. EDWARDS.

Col Britton Mr. R. STANTON—Frederick Mr. CLEATHER

Gibby Mr. G STANTON—Liffardo Mr. DUNN,

Alguzile Mr MARTIN,

Vasques Mr. LONG

Violante Miss. MELLON,

Isabella Mrs. R. STANTON,—Flora Mrs. EDWARDS

Inis Mrs. DUNN,

Singing by Meffrs Craneson Martin and Dunn,

To which will be added a Favourite ENTERTAINMENT call'd

No Song no Supper.

Robin Mr R. STANTON,

Frederick Mr. MARTIN—Crop Mr. CRANESON,

Endless Mr DUNN—William Mr G STANTON,

Sailors Mr CLEATHER, Mr LONG Mr. KELD,&c

Margaretta Miss MELLON—Louisa Mrs DUNN.

Dorothy Mrs EDWARDS—Nelly Mrs. MITTEER.

Boxes 3s.----Pit and upper Slips 2s.----Gallery 1s.

Places for the Boxes to taken of Mr. R. Stanton, at the Theatre
from Eleven 'till One.

It is requested Ladies and Gentlemen will take Tickets for the number of Places wanted, and send Servants early to keep them.

To begin at Half Past Six,

The Company perform every Evening this Week.

FOR THE BENEFIT OF

Mr. SMITH.

Who respectfully solicits the Patronage of the Ladies and Gentlemen of STAFFORD and its Vicinity.

THEATRE STAFFORD.

On THURSDAY Evening, the 16th JANUARY, 1817,

Will be presented, SHAKESPEARE's celebrated Tragedy of

MACBETH

KING OF SCOTLAND.

WITH ALL THE ORIGINAL MUSIC, CHORUSSES, INCANTATIONS, &c.

Macbeth, Mr. SMITH.—Macduff, Mr. SEYMOUR.—Banquo, Mr. FAWCETT.—Duncan, Mr. FAIRBAIRN.
Malcolm, Mr. COLLIER.—Lenox, Mr. HENDERSON.—Seyton, Mr. PRITCHARD.
Fleance, Master STANTON.—Ross, Mr. DAVIES.—Messengers, Messrs. BATIGAN, and LOCKINGTON.
Lady Macbeth, Miss PHILLIPS.—Lady in Waiting, Mrs. FAIRBAIRN.
Hecate, Mr. ROWLANDS.
Singing Witches, Miss WESTON & Miss ROWLANDS.—Speaking Witches, Mrs. FAWCETT & Mrs. ROWLANDS.

This excellent Piece commences with

The EXECUTION of the THANE of CAWDOR.

And the Treacherous Prognostics of the WEIRD SISTERS.

The Barbarous MURDER of their good old KING DUNCAN.

THE CORONATION OF MACBETH,

The Assassination of Banquo, and the Appearance of his GHOST at the Royal Banquet.

HECATE'S CAVE.

A Dance of Witches round the Burning Cauldron.

Into which the Evil Spirits throw their Charms and Magic Spells.

AND THE SEVERAL APPARITIONS OF EIGHT KINGS.

END OF THE PLAY,

A COMIC SONG, by Mr. PRITCHARD.

DANCING,

By Miss ROWLANDS and Mr. COLLIER.

AND A SONG, BY MR. BATIGAN.

The whole to conclude with the laughable FARCE of, The

WEATHERCOCK.

Tristram Fickle, Mr. SMITH.
Old Fickle, Mr. ROWLANDS.—Briefwit, Mr. FAIRBAIRN.—Sneer, Mr. PRITCHARD.
Gardener, Mr. HENDERSON.—John, Mr. COLLIER.—Barber, Mr. BATIGAN.
Variella, Miss H. PHILLIPS.—Ready, Miss WESTON.

BOXES 3s.——PIT 2s.——GALLERY 1s.

☞ TICKETS to be had of Mr. SMITH, at Mr. Meeson's, in the Gaol-Gate Street, and of Mr. MORGAN, Printer.

THEATRE, STAFFORD.

Mr. STANTON has the pleasure to gratify his Patrons with the Performance of
THE CELEBRATED

MASTER BURKE,

A CHILD ONLY NINE YEARS OF AGE!

Whose surprising abilities in TRAGEDY, COMEDY, and MUSIC, have astonished and delighted the London Audience. He is now on a Tour to the Principal Country Theatres, and will perform on FRIDAY the Second, and SATURDAY the Third of January; being THE ONLY NIGHTS he can appear here, from his numerous previous Engagements. Notwithstanding the HEAVY EXPENCE OF HIS ENGAGEMENT, the Price of Admission will be as usual, BOXES 3s.—PIT, 2s. GALLERY, 1s but nothing under FULL PRICE can be taken during his performance here.

On FRIDAY EVENING, JANUARY 2nd, 1829,
Will be presented Macklin's admired Comedy, of

Love a la Mode.

Sir CALLAGHAN O'BRALLAGHAN, by MASTER BURKE,

In which Character he will Sing the original Song,
"Let Other Men Sing of their Goddesses Bright."
Sir Archy Mc Sarcasm, Mr. SHELDON.—Sir Theodore Goodchild, Mr. FAIRBAIRN.
Mordecai, Mr. MAITLAND.—Squire Groom, Mr. HALLAM.
Thomas, Mr. ECCLES.
Charlotte, Miss H. STANTON.

In the course of the Evening,
Master BURKE will sing, for the first time, a New Song, illustrative of

Breaking up for Christmas Holidays

OR, THE YOUNG LADIES BOARDING SCHOOL PLAY!

In which he will give imitations of the Governess—The Parents—A French Teacher, who is Directress of the Play—Little Girl, as Prologue—Lisping Girl, as Hamlet—Frightened Little Girl, as Macbeth—Swearing Girl, as Motley—Whining Girl, as Richard, &c. &c. &c.

Master BURKE will lead the Orchestra, in ROSSINI's

Overture to Tancredi,

As performed by him in London, to crowded and enraptured Audiences.

Singing, by Mrs. Sheldon, Mr. Sheldon, Mr. Hallam, & Mr. Wood

To conclude with a Drama, written expressly for Master Burke, as performed in London with enthusiastic Applause entitled

A Day after the Fair

Or, The COTTAGE by the ROAD SIDE.

Old Fidget, (a retired Stock Broker)........................ by Mr. BROMLEY.
Clod, (a Yorkshire Servant)............................... Mr. HALLAM.
Jerry, (Mr. Sterling's Servant)........................... Master BURKE!
Sam Wax, (a Drunken Cobbler,)............................. Master BURKE!!
Sarah Squall, (a Ballad Singer,).......................... Master BURKE!!
Timothy Thumpaway, (a Drummer,)........................... Master BURKE!!
Mademoiselle Dumpling, (a Bravura Singer,)................ Master BURKE!!
With a SONG, half Italian half French, called "The PETIT MARMOT."
Octavius Moonshine, (a Madman,)........................... Master BURKE !!!!!
Polly, Servant at the Cottage,.......................... Mrs. SHELDON!
Madame Maypole, a Manageress............................ Mrs. SHELDON!!
Sukey Scrub, a Washerwoman.............................. Mrs. SHELDON!!!

TICKETS to be had of Mr. MORGAN, Bookseller, where Places in the Boxes may be taken.
☞ Doors to be opened at Half-past SIX o'Clock, and the Performance to begin at SEVEN.

On SATURDAY, Master BURKE will perform the Character of TEDDY O'ROUKE, Sing several original Songs, written expressly for him, Play several Airs on the Violin, and Perform the Principal Character in the Farce.—This Night will be for the BENEFIT of Master BURKE, and positively the LAST NIGHT of His Performing here.

MORGAN, PRINTER, STAFFORD.

THEATRE, STAFFORD.

The MANAGER anxious to gratify the Patrons of the Drama, has the honor of announcing

FOR TWO NIGHTS ONLY,

The most singular Novelty in the Theatrical World,

An Actor of Colour !!!

Known throughout America and England by the appellation of the

AFRICAN ROSCIUS,

His success in New York, and the principal Theatres in the United States, has induced him to visit England professionally. He is engaged by the proprietors of the THEATRE ROYAL COVENT GARDEN, on which stage he will make his first appearance early in the present season, previously to which he has visited the principal Theatres in the Kingdom, viz. Bath, Bristol, Brighton, Liverpool, Manchester, Edinburgh, Glasgow, &c. in each place his extraordinary efforts have been witnessed with astonishment by brilliant and crowded Audiences.

On MONDAY Evening, December 20th, 1830,

Will be presented, Shakespeare's admired Tragedy of

OTHELLO,

Moor of Venice.

The Part of OTHELLO, (Moor of Venice) by the
AFRICAN ROSCIUS.

END OF THE PLAY.

A Favorite Song, by Mrs. PHILLIPS,
AND A COMIC SONG, BY MR. PHILLIPS.

To conclude with the admired New Farce, (never acted here) of

POPPING the QUESTION

OPPOSITE LEFT: This 1817 playbill tells the story of Macbeth *in such detail that it was hardly worthwhile going to the theatre to see it. RIGHT: Master Burke was one of the many 'infant' prodigies' to perform in Martin Street. ABOVE LEFT: This appearance of the African Roscius as Othello was one of the Martin Street theatre's failures. (All WSL)*

RIGHT: The Playhouse (1912). The original theatre in Martin Street (then called Smokey Lane) was built by Samuel Stanton in 1792, and was first called the Lyceum in 1848. (PR) OPPOSITE BELOW: The fire brigade in 1906. (SH&CS) LEFT: The fire station in 1961, adjoining the Royal Brine Baths. (Mrs Dav)   RIGHT: A 1913 fire engine. (EH)

LEFT: The ill-fated Sandonia, on its opening as a theatre in 1920 (BS) and RIGHT: in its present role as a Bingo Hall. BELOW: The Picture House in 1931. (An annual Outing)

LEFT: The interior of the Albert Hall cinema in 1925.
(SCCM) RIGHT: The Gatehouse Theatre.
BELOW: The Odeon Cinema, opened by the Earl
of Shrewsbury in 1936, and taken over by the
Astra Film Centre in 1981.

A model of the Titfield Thunderbolt, constructed by W.G. Bagnall Ltd, the locomotive builders, advertising the film of that name at the Odeon in the mid-50s. The Alexandra Hotel and the clocktower of the Royal Brine Baths (both of which were to become victims of the Town Planners) can be seen in the background.

THE DEMON DRINK

In the 19th century, drunkenness was a serious social problem. The public houses of the 1840s anticipated the proud slogan of the Windmill Theatre during the blitz a hundred years later: 'We Never Closed'; and, as a consequence, drunkenness was rife, particularly amongst what was then known as the 'lower classes'. Everybody was aware of the problem but, although there was much debate and public protest, little was done to solve it. We are familiar with the type of illustration so often seen in those hypocritical Victorian days: the cruel father slumped over the kitchen table in a drunken stupor, empty beer bottles strewn about the floor, his distraught wife kneeling at his feet, ragged infants clutching at her skirts. Even the local theatre got into the act, no doubt in the pious hope that its contribution to social reform might help to fill empty seats and provide the extra cash the box office so sorely needed. *The Bottle*, produced at the Martin Street Lyceum in March 1848, is a typical example. 'A Moral Drama', screamed the playbills, 'fraught with moral and salutary lessons . . . The Career of a Drunkard, every Inordinate Cup is unblessed and its Ingredient The Devil'.

In fact, two of the local inns, the Blue Post and the White Hart, catered especially for the theatrical profession. A favourite rendezvous of the players at the Lyceum, the Blue Post was only two doors away from the theatre — those of Parker's pork shop and the Fountain Inn. Harry and Mary Thompson, the proprietors of the Blue Post at the turn of the century, were music hall artistes; and in his fascinating book *Working the Halls*, their great-grandson Peter Honri — himself a well known 'concertinist entertainer — describes the old music hall which his family did so much to keep alive but which now, alas, is gone for ever. He tells of the excitement in Stafford at the news of the relief of Mafeking, when 'the fair [does] a roaring trade, especially the coconut shy where favourite targets are the Boars' leaders' heads . . . and the Lyceum Theatre is patriotically decorated to match the Blue Post'. Just round the corner, in Eastgate Street, the White Hart Inn also served as a theatrical boarding house, patronised by the performers at the Martin Street theatre and the Albert Hall, in Crabbery Street. Again, the licenceee, Mrs Bodie, was a member of a family well known in the music hall: Tom (alias 'Dr' Walford) Bodie, 'magician, hypnotist and ventriloquist', with his Kaiser Bill moustache, was one of the most highly paid entertainers of his day. On the night of 4 June 1915, the White Hart played its part in a scene of excitement and heroism to match anything performed on the Lyceum stage. This was the night when the theatre (then called The Playhouse) was gutted by fire, and P. Hamilton-Jones, the business manager of the current touring company, was staying at the inn. On the outbreak of the fire, he dressed hurriedly and rushed over to the theatre, where he crossed the blazing stage and, at considerable personal risk, tried to retrieve some of the company's property from the dressing rooms. Overcome by smoke, he narrowly escaped serious injury when part of the roof collapsed, before he was carried from the burning building.

Words of warning about the Demon Drink came from more responsible sources than the stage of the Lyceum. 'The evil effects of drink', said Mr Justice Fry, at Stafford Assizes in 1878, '. . . ought to make everyone ask himself — are we using our influence to the utmost to diminish this source of evil and misery?' The answer, of course, was that 'we' were not, as that distinguished do-gooder, Prime Minister W.E. Gladstone, made clear in a speech to the House of Commons on 5 March 1880: 'It has been said', he pointed out, 'that greater calamities are inflicted on mankind by intemperance than by the three great historical scourges — war, pestilence and famine. That is true, and it is the measure of our disgrace'.

Stafford was no better and no worse than other towns, and a lighthearted reminder of its inebriate days can still be seen in Lichfield Road where the old lockup, a stone, dungeonlike structure, has been preserved in much the same condition as it was when the local drunks spent an uncomfortable night there, before an even more uncomfortable 'morning after' in the pillory or the stocks. For a time, the county town not only had its fair share of drunks, but of breweries to satisfy their needs, though brewing, as an industry, never had anything more than a local significance. The Stafford Brewery, established in Foregate Street in the 1840s, survived only some twenty years. Two others came upon the scene in the 1860s, one in South Walls, the other on The Green in Forebridge, but neither lasted long and by the turn of the century both had been absorbed by Eley's (Stafford) Brewery. The end came in 1928, when Eley's themselves were taken over by Butler's of Wolverhampton, and closed by them in the same year. In fact, one of the small, privately owned breweries outlived them all. Attached to the Princess Royal in Sandon Road, it had been opened in the 1850s by the Dawson brothers, members of a well known Stafford family, and thereafter Dawson's Home Brewed Ale was a popular local drink for nearly a century, until the brewery finally closed a few years after the end of the Second World War.

Though the breweries were shortlived, there was no lack of licensed houses in the town: in 1852, there were 86 in the borough alone (23 of them being beer houses), nearly half of them in and around the town centre. With ten to its credit, Eastgate Street was particularly well served, and remained so into the present century. When I was living with my parents over their shop in Salter Street (a continuation of Eastgate Street) during the 1914–1918 war, there were seven within little more than a hundred yards of us — the Vine, the Rose and Crown, the Sheridan, the White Hart, the Castle, the Cow and Hare and the Shrewsbury Arms. Drunken brawls were the order of the day — or rather, night, particularly Saturday night. Though the protagonists rarely suffered anything worse than a black eye or a night in the police cells for those who preferred it to an angry wife awaiting them at home, a rolling pin at the ready, I once saw near/murder done by a young soldier on leave from the horrors of war: I can remember to this day the sound of his bayonet clattering to the pavement when he was disarmed by one of his companions.

Apart from supplying their quota of tenants for the Lichfield Road lockup, some of the licensed houses form an integral part of the town's history; three of them, dating from the 17th century, in Greengate Street, within a few yards of each other. Said to have been erected on the ruins of the old college buildings of St Mary's Church, proof of the antiquity of the Swan Hotel came to light as recently as July 1946, when a 'priests' hole' was discovered, concealed in an upstairs room. Staffordians of my generation can remember when the Swan still looked like the coaching inn it had once been, its arched, cobblestoned entrance leading to the stables at the rear, where George Borrow once groomed the horses; and guests could still be directed to the bedroom where Charles I had slept when it formed part of the Ancient High House where he and Prince Rupert stayed in September 1642, a few weeks after the commencement of the Civil War.

Borrow thought highly of the inn, which he described in *Romany Rye* as 'a place of infinite life and bustle . . . with an army of servants . . . when lonely and melancholy I have called upon the time I spent there and never failed to become cheerful from the recollection'. Charles Dickens took a different view of what he called 'the extinct town inn, "the Dodo" . . . which has seen better days . . . has nothing in the larder . . . is narrowminded as to towels [and] expects me to wash on a Freemason's apron without the trimming'. He didn't think much of the town either — 'as dull and dead a town as anyone could not desire to see'. Daniel Defoe, the earliest of the trio of distinguished authors, had felt much the same about the county town a century earlier. After visiting Lichfield, 'with its good conversation and good company', he found Stafford a disappointment when he made a detour to call there, an opinion shared by others who found it 'a dull, idle place' . . . 'very mean, though the county town'. Lord Campbell, then a barrister on the Oxford Circuit, capped the lot with his terse verdict: 'The dullest and vilest town in England'. Though one of the most eminent lawyers of his day and a future Lord Chief Justice, Campbell's parliamentary record was less than distinguished, if a local solicitor named Webb is to be believed. When giving evidence before a Select Committee of the House of Lords in 1833, he deposed to having paid 531 of the 556 electors for the votes they cast in the 1830 Election for the then Sir John Campbell.

As the disillusioned Mr Dickens gazed moodily out of the Swan window, one wonders what he thought about the inn across the road, its bear standing proudly over the entrance as it still does today. Almost as old as its more famous neighbour, the original site of the Bear Inn formed part of St Chad's churchyard. It was then the Black Bear, but by 1818 it had changed colour and become the White Bear, from which coaches started on their journeys to London and Birmingham. It is mentioned for the first time without any reference to its colour, in White's Directory of 1851, and it was simply the Bear Inn which was finally taken over and reconstructed by Eley's Brewery in 1882.

The Alexandra Hotel, the third, and architecturally the most beautiful of the ancient trio, was to become one of the more notable victims of the local town planners. Originally built by the Whitby family as their town house, with its dormer windows, its sloping, roofed forecourt, its oak-panelled interior and magnificent staircase, it was one of the town's finest mansions. It remained virtually unchanged when it was converted into an hotel, and was made the subject of a preservation order when it closed in 1961. But the planners knew better; the building was demolished two years later, and suffered its final indignity when it was replaced by a supermarket.

Other old inns demand mention. Adjoining the 18th century lockup, the White Lion, built in the 1660s, was believed to occupy the site of the Hospital of St John the Baptist, but later discoveries suggest that the hospital of the Middle Ages was situated further north, somewhere between the Grapes Inn and the Green Bridge.

Little is known of the early history of the premises in Crabbery Street which became the Noah's Ark. That they were originally built as a residence of the Dean of St Mary's may or may not be true, but it is reasonably certain that Elizabeth I called there on her way to the Castle when she visited the town in 1575. Most of the original half-timbered building, with its projecting porch, disappeared when the premises were rebuilt in the 1890s; when the Corporation decided not to renew the brewery's lease in 1966, the premises where Good Queen Bess had 'taken wine' nearly four hundred years earlier, were converted into offices and now house those for consumer protection.

The Grand Junction Hotel and Posting House in Newport Road (later known simply as the Junction, until its closure in 1965) had the doubtful privilege of enjoying the custom of the only local felon to earn a place in Madam Tussaud's Chamber of Horrors. While staying at the Grand Junction, William Palmer, the Rugeley poisoner, attempted to murder one Tom Myatts whom he believed was ready to spill the beans about one of his criminal escapades. But 'the Prince of Poisoners', so experienced in the art of murder, was not up to his usual form. Although his drink had been generously laced with poison, Myatts survived to see Palmer publicly hanged outside the prison in Gaol Road on 14 June 1856, before a crowd estimated to number 30,000.

On a more comic note, the chief claim to fame of the Abercrombie Inn lies in its association with a Society whose founders obviously had a sense of humour as well as a partiality for ale. Opened in 1830, off Gaol Square, the Abercrombie was the headquarters of the Reformed Order of Odd Women, with a membership of 100 thirsty 'Sisters'. Determined to survive as long as an abnormal intake of alcohol permitted, these resourceful dowagers had their own surgeon in attendance, who agreed to present them with six gallons of ale on his appointment, and thereafter to attend them for a quarter, free of charge. The only male member of the Order was its secretary, who received the princely salary of 15s per quarter, plus a share of the aforesaid ale. This improbable Society moved later to Cock Inn in Eastgate, and finally to the Three Tuns in Gaolgate Street. History does not record whether the surgeon and secretary accompanied them. Though deprived of the custom of the alcoholic Sisters, the Abercrombie outlived them and finally closed its doors in March 1959.

The alcoholic scene has changed a lot over the years. The number of public houses has been substantially reduced, licensing hours have shortened, the price of beer and spirits has risen astronomically, and the only drunks who can still afford to qualify as a public menace are those who drive cars. Around 75 licensed houses have closed in as many years, and it must surely be more than coincidence that these should include all the 'Jolly' ones — the Jolly Potter, the Jolly Crafts, the Jolly Bacchus, and (who could devise a better name?) the Jolly Toper.

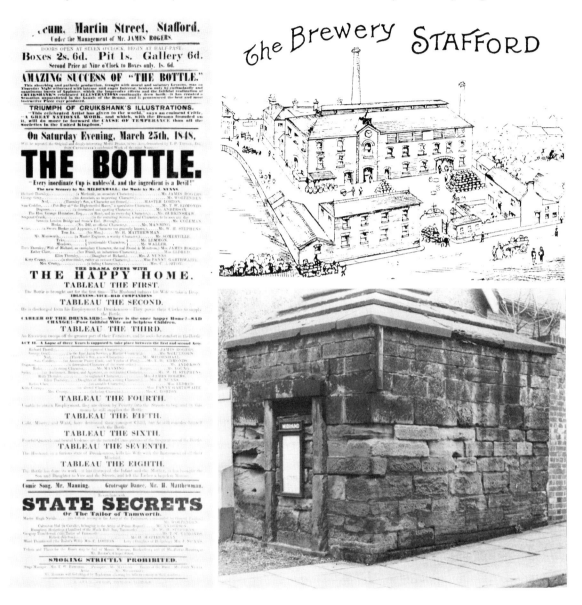

LEFT: Playbill of The Bottle *(1848), at the Lyceum Theatre, condemning the Demon Drink. (WSL) ABOVE: Stafford Brewery (c1850). (CE) BELOW: The lock-up, overnight resting place for local drunks. (WSL)*

ELEY'S
Stafford Brewery, Ltd.

THE BREWERY, STAFFORD,

BREWERS, MALTSTERS,

— AND —

WINE AND SPIRIT
❧ MERCHANTS.

	Per Brl.	Per Kil.	Per Fir.	Per Gall.
A.K. Light Bitter Ale	36/-	18/-	9/-	1/-
No. 1 X Mild Ale	36/-	18/-	9/-	1/-
No. 2 XX Excellent Dinner Ale	42/-	21/-	10/6	1/2
No. 3 XXX Superior	48/-	24/-	12/-	1/4
No. 4 XXXX Strong Ale	54/-	27/-	13/6	1/6
No. 5 XXXXX Strong Ale	60/-	30/-	15/-	1/8
EX. Finest Strong Ale	72/-	36/-	18/-	2/-
I.P.A.—India Pale Ale	54/-	27/-	13/6	1/6
Stout	48/-	24/-	12/-	1/4

**Beer from 6d. to 10d. per gall.
Supplied in 9, 18, 36, and 54 Gallon Casks.**

ELEY'S SPECIAL STAFFORD STOUT.

Firkins of 9 Gallons	**13/6**
Small Bottles, about ½-pint	**2/-** per doz.
Large ,, (reputed pints)	**3/-** ,,

All the above are guaranteed Pure and Genuine, made from the best
materials, and contain no hop substitutes or other adulterants.

*LEFT: Eley's Brewery's price list, guaranteed to turn the modern drinker green with envy.
ABOVE: Dawson's Home-Brewed Ale was a popular local drink for almost q century. (Both CE)
RIGHT: The Police Station in Market Square (1933). (SH&CS)*

ABOVE: The present Police Station in Eastgate Street, on the site of Izaak Walton's birthplace.
BELOW: The Castle and the White Hart in Eastgate Street.(c1877). (SH&CS)

OPPOSITE ABOVE: Horse Fair outside the White Hart (1911). (WSL) BELOW: The Swan Hotel, Greengate Street (c1910), (WSL) and LEFT: a Swan advertisement (1906). RIGHT: The Fox and George and the Sheridan in Eastgate Street (c1904). (SH&CS) BELOW: The Alexandra Hotel advertisement (1906).

LEFT: The Alexandra Hotel, Greengate Street, before falling victim to the town planners and being replaced by a supermarket. (PR) RIGHT: The Bear Inn, Greengate Street. BELOW: The White Lion Inn, and adjoining lock-up, in Lichfield Road (c1843). (WSL)

ABOVE: The White Lion in 1906, demolished in 1970 to make way for a traffic island. (SH & CS)
BELOW: The Grand Junction Commercial Hotel and Posting House, in Newport Road (c1860).
(WSL)

LEFT: The Roebuck Inn, at the junction of Greengate Street and St Martin's Lane (now Martin Street) (c1860). BELOW: The Noah's Ark Inn, Crabbery Street, where Elizabeth I is said to have 'taken wine' on her way to the Castle in 1575. RIGHT: The Maid's Head Inn, (c1840) Gaolgate Street. (All WSL)

LEFT: The Vine Hotel, RIGHT: the Jolly Crafts Inn, (Mrs Dy) and BELOW: an outing from the Prince Albert Inn (c1928). (WSL)

ABOVE: A Sunday School centenary (1900). (WSL) BELOW: An Infirmary Pageant before the 1914–18 war. (SCCM)

ETHELFLEDA'S LEGACY

Those of my generation have probably seen more changes and a greater advance in human knowledge than any other period of history. When I was born, the motor car was a near farcical curiosity, its driver and passenger muffled, begloved figures of fun, the aeroplane little more than an elaborate, highly dangerous kite, piloted by lunatics who held life cheap. The world was vast and, for most of us, unexplored; and anyone who had dared suggest that, before the century was out, man would have invaded outer space and walked on the moon, would have been led away to some quiet retreat for the mentally deranged. But man has been too clever for his own good, and ever since he split the atom, the mushroom cloud of the atomic bomb has loomed menacingly over mankind, threatening its very existence.

Stafford, like other towns of its kind, has enjoyed — and suffered — the fruits of progress. Though it lacked many of the advantages it enjoys today, the sleepy market town in which I spent my youth was a safer, comfortable place where life was lived at a more leisurely pace; there were no petrol fumes to invade your nostrils, children could spin their tops and bowl their hoops in the street, quite safely, and dad could go to a football match without risk to life and limb. You made your own amusements in those days, when radio was in its infancy and there was no television to keep a man chained, goggle-eyed, to his armchair. Card games were a favourite pastime, with whist at the top of the list. Whist Drives (sometimes even the luxury of a Whist Drive *and* Dance, 3s/6d, including refreshments, Premier Prize, a bicycle!) were as popular then as bingo is today, and made greater demands on the intelligence. Some of those events were organised on an ambitious scale. I remember one in particular, held in aid of St Dunstan's, the society for the blind, when preliminary rounds were played in the provinces, the winners taking part in the Grand Final, in London, with a First Prize of £1,000, which was once won by a Stafford man. The musical evening at home was another popular occasion and, if you grew tired of listening to uncle Fred singing *Friend o' Mine* or uncle George reciting *The Green Eye Of The Little Yellow God*, you could always go to 'the pictures' and nine penn'orth of Pearl White.

In his *History of and Guide to Stafford*, Charles Calvert describes the county town he knew when he was Librarian of the Free Library and Curator of the Wragge Museum in 1886: 'The town possesses many marks of former ages in its half-timbered houses whose fanciful fronts have been carefully preserved, and generally bears an appearance of respectability, from its handsome shops, extensive and commodious hotels, genteel residences and elegant public buildings, all of which bear evidence of the great improvement and progress which has taken place since the time when Dickens visited Stafford and recorded his impressions of it. Some of its churches are also worthy of remark for their antiquity, and in its vicinity are several mansions of the nobility and gentry,

101

Sandon Hall (the seat of . . . the Earl of Harrowby), Tixall and Ingestre Hall (. . . the Earl of Shrewsbury and Talbot), Shugborough Hall (. . . the Earl of Lichfield) . . . as a remnant of the feudal grandeur may be seen on a conical eminence at a distance of about a mile to the south west, the ruins of the castle of the renouned Barons of Stafford . . . Stafford is one of the most important railway centres in the L. & N.W. system . . . population . . . is over 20,000'.

How different is the town of today. The 'several mansions' (and the railway station) have survived, but the 'nobility and gentry', crippled by taxation, have had to resort to various money-raising devices to keep a roof over their noble heads. While the stately homes and their environs have thus been preserved, the town centre has not been so fortunate. Old inns like the Swan and the Bear still remain, and the Ancient High House and Chetwynd House have managed to escape the axe of the planners, but the 'handsome shops' and 'genteel residences' have gone, and the main street which I knew as a boy has changed beyond recognition. Not only have nearly all the old shops disappeared: the Royal Brine Baths have accompanied them into oblivion. Gone are the days when you could hire a boat or a canoe, for sixpence an hour, from 'Old Joe', the irascible old man in charge of the Green Bridge Boathouse, and row or paddle your way to the Ladder Bridge. There was nothing particularly beautiful about the Baths building, nor was it very old but, like Old Joe, it had character and, when it was demolished in 1977, one of the last remaining landmarks of the old town had gone, to be replaced by an enormous office block and two supermarkets, on the north and south banks of the Sow. Small wonder that the river which halted the Danes a thousand years ago looks so depressed today: an invader would hardly get his feet wet in its shallow, reed-ridden waters, and nothing remains to remind us of its past save a solitary, disillusioned swan, staring disapprovingly at the half-submerged supermarket trollies thrown into it by anonymous, mindless morons.

That the town has improved as a shopping centre is beyond argument. The new precinct between Crabbery Street and Gaol Square provides a wider range of merchandise for the customer and, while the supermarkets lack the family atmosphere of the old shops whose proprietors were often personal friends, they have more to offer. It is not the facilities they provide which causes concern, but the deterioration in the appearance of the main street which their invasion has caused and for which the town planners must shoulder much of the blame: little attempt has been made to harmonise the new buildings with the old ones they have spared. The result is something of an architectural nightmare with remnants of the past, like the High House and the beautiful old Norman Church of St Chad relegated to the role of intruders on the modern scene, as ill-fitting as a cathedral on Blackpool's Golden Mile.

Though the savaging of the main street was to come later, the approach to the town from the railway station was improved at the turn of the century. When Mr R.C. Lambert (affectionately remembered as 'Billy' by those Old Edwardians who were taught maths by him) arrived there on an autumn evening in 1903, to take up his appointment at the Grammar School, the first view he had of the town where he was to spend the rest of his life was what he thought was an ornamental lake, 'which looked rather striking with the lights of the few lamps reflected in it'. He was soon to be disillusioned. When he engaged a four-wheeler to complete his journey (whose driver looked 'rather surprised', since the school was only a few yards away), he realised that his lake was, in fact, 'a piece of waste ground covered with bricks, broken bottles and refuse of all kinds'.

Billy did not have to wait long to see an improvement. In 1908, some four acres of marshland were raised by three feet to reduce the danger of flooding, and Billy's brick-strewn desert was converted into Victoria Pleasure Gardens. The Pleasure Gardens (now Victoria Park) were introduced to the public with a surprising lack of fuss: there was no formal opening, and the only function held to celebrate such a major improvement was an evening concert by the Band of the North Staffs Regiment. Described in the press as 'a great boon to the town [which] will be highly appreciated by the residents', the new Park, with the river lapping gently through its grassy banks, had a natural beauty which the Severn Trent Water Authority recently purported to improve, at considerable cost. Whether they succeeded is, to say the least, doubtful.

When looking back, one is always inclined to remember the good and forget the bad; while it is natural that the older generation should regret the passing of the days of their youth, many of the changes they have lived to see have been for the better. Poverty was rife in 'the good old days' before the Welfare State, and examples of it could be seen, not only at the north end but in the centre of the town. North and South Walls — then known simply as Back Walls — was a slum, with sacking over the broken windows of dilapidated terraced houses, half-naked children sitting on the doorsteps, no shoes to their feet and scabs of malnutrition on their pallid little faces — and, within 100 yards of the main street, a dosshouse, straight out of Dickens. Every generation, including our own, has its cases of genuine hardship, but the vast majority of those who now complain of their standard of living (colour television and all) would do well to look to the conditions in which their grandparents lived, and count their blessings.

A visitor's first impression of the county town of today will depend largely on whether he travels by train or by car. If he chooses the former and manages to ignore the office block which has replaced the houses and the Station Hotel in Victoria Road, he will be persuaded that he is approaching a town of considerable charm. On leaving the railway station, he will cross the river bridge, see Victoria Park on his right and, ahead of him, St Mary's Church (which has been described, accurately enough, as a cathedral without a bishop) towering over Victoria Square, with the War Memorial in its centre. A few years ago, disillusion came after he had crossed the quiet churchyard and found himself confronted by a main street congested with noisy, slow-moving traffic, and apprehensive pedestrians trying to decide when they dare take their lives in their hands and cross the road. The visitor of the 1980s has been spared this ordeal by the relief road which was commenced in 1976. Running from Gaol Square to Lichfield Road, trespassing over the site of the royal fish pool on its way, it has drained the town centre of its heavy traffic, and the shoppers who use it no doubt echo Francisco's words on the battlements at Elsinore — 'For this relief, much thanks'.

103

Not so the unsuspecting motorist visiting Stafford for the first time: what he is likely to say as he enters the maze of approach roads, with their surfeit of bewildering signs and traffic lights, is unprintable. We are frequently assured by Jimmy Saville, on the television screen, that this is 'the age of the train', and he might well be right. Anyone contemplating a visit to the county town would be well advised to heed his words before driving his car out of the garage.

ABOVE: King Edward VII at Shugborough in 1907. (SCCM) BELOW: Edward, Prince of Wales, later King Edward VIII, at the railway station in 1928. (Mr N) OPPOSITE ABOVE: Market Square, Coronation of George VI. (Mrs M) LEFT: Shugborough Hall. BELOW: Ingestre Hall; RIGHT: Sandon Hall. (all WSL)

105

105

ABOVE: The Council Chamber in 1906. BELOW: A Mayoral group of the same date. OPPOSITE: Thomas Cox, the 1906 Town Crier. (All SH&CS)

ABOVE: Horses and trap being driven past the Grammar School in Newport Road, (c1900).
CENTRE: A family outing (c1915). BELOW: Mason's brake (c1920). (Mrs S)

ABOVE: A funeral hearse of the 1920s. (SCCM) BELOW: Attwood's Ford cars display, County Show (1920s). (BS)

ABOVE: Boating on the Sow in the 1920s. BELOW: The Ladder Bridge.

LEFT: R.C. Lambert, MA and RIGHT: Victoria Park (opened in 1908). BELOW: Unveiling of the War Memorial in Victoria Square (1922). (WSL) OPPOSITE ABOVE: St Chad's Church,(WSL) and BELOW: the Royal Brine Baths (c1924). (WSL)

BIBLIOGRAPHY

Calvert, Charles. *A History of and Guide to Stafford*, published by J. Halden & Son, Stafford, 1886.

Hibbert, Cecil. *A Handbook and Guide to Stafford*, published by Brookfields, Stafford, 1906.

Horne, J. Sidney. *Notes for a History of King Edward VI School, Stafford*, published by R. W. Hourd & Son, Stafford, 1930.

Gilmore, C.G. MA, PhD, *History of King Edward VI School, Stafford*, published by Oxford University Press, 1953.

Butters, Paul. *Cinderella Story: A History of Stafford Rangers F.C.*, published by Hourdsprint, Stafford, 1972.

Butters, Paul. *Stafford: The Story of a Thousand Years*, published by The Crescent Publishing Co, 1979.

Honri, Peter. *Working the Halls*, first published by Saxon House, 1973.

Lewis, Roy and Anslow, Joan. *Stafford As It Was*, Published by Hendon Publishing Co Ltd, 1980.

Staffs County Council. *Stafford Remembered*, published by Staffs CC Education Dept, 1982.

Greenslade, M.W., Johnson, D.A., & Currie, C.R.J. *A History of Stafford*, reprinted by Staffordshire County Library from *The Victoria History of the County of Stafford,* 1982.

Gordon, John F. *The Staffordshire Bull Terrier.*

INDEX

113

114

SUBSCRIBERS

Presentation Copies

1   Stafford Borough Council
2   Staffordshire County Council
3   William Salt Library
4   The Stafford Newsletter
5   Stafford Historical & Civic Society
6   The Gatehouse Theatre

7   Paul Butters
8   Clive & Carolyn Birch
9   A.L. Lowe
10 Mrs P. Macdonald
11 S. G. Macdonald
12 A. Cartwright
13 J.B. Taylor
14
15 John Fiddler
16 W.P.T. Watson
17 J.N. Woolcock
18 J.T. Tucker
19 T.D. Nowell
20 J.R. Barnsley
21 Mrs L. Turner
22
23 A.J. Carwardine
24 Cedric Arthur Pickin
25 Gordon Brookes
26 S.M. Howard
27 J. Nicholas
28 James H. Simpson
29 David W. Slee
30 Sydney Pearson
31 Paul Dale
32 C.C. Lee
33 J. Ian McOwan
34 John Wood
35 R. Canavon
36 Mrs M. J. Wilkinson
37 Mrs J. Lowbridge
38 David G. Ashton
39
41 Staffordshire County Library
42 Malcolm George
43 J.V. Hodgens
44 Ray Roberts
       (Booksellers) of
       Whitson
45 R.M. Holmes
46 G. Steventon
47 T. Jennings
48 Mrs M.W. Wright
49 Dyrick A. Hughes
50 Chris Ingram
51 K.J. Walker
52 M Powell
53 D. Lovatt
54 Derek W. Booth
55 S.D.L. Silver
56 Peter Newbold
57 R. Thomas
58 J.R. & D.A. Wilson
59 S.W. Smith

60 Miss Nina Spurr
61 H. Rellinger-Stafford
62 Ernest J. Aston
63 Eric William Barlow
64 R.N. Buxton OBE BEM QPM
65
66 Mrs B.M. Glass
67 Brian H. Linford
68 Dr John Pegg
69
83 Staffordshire County Council
84 Gordon Pickin
85 Margaret Hill
86 Charles Vernon
87 James W. Flower
88 Roderick Lainton
89 Roy Mitchell
90 Mrs D. Rimmer
91 M. Dudley
92 Margaret M. Martin
93 Betty L. Brown
94 N. Felton
95 Betty Morris
96 Mr & Mrs M.J. Dixon
97 P.A. Leason
98 Mrs Pennington
99 R.E. Bayley
100 L. Crutchley
101 A.E. Glover
102 C.F. Tidey
103 Fred Allen
104 Arthur Bowen
105 R.L. McNaughton
106 T. Bruce
107 Mrs J Allen
108 Paul N.A. Baker
109 Mrs Olive Boyles
110 R. Mudway
111 Scott Humphrey
112 Mrs M. Beal
113 A.M. Yale
114 Claire Blakemore
115 F.L. Walk
116 Kathleen Wise
117 E. Flavell
118 Mrs R.H. Critchley
119 E. Grattage
120 Mavis Bird
121 Richard A.J. Nixon
122 W.J. Bradshaw
123 Stephen Paul Green
124 M.W. Tomkinson
125 Rev Dr J.D. Young
126 R.C.F. Clayton

127 Richard Homer
128 Mrs R.J. Jenkinson
129 G. Hughes
130 M.M. Raftery
131
134 S.H.C. Wade
135 K. Johnson
136 Mrs Jean Simpson
137 R.E. Turner
138 Pauline Bevans
139
140 Mrs Lucy Hill
141 Rosemary Mellor
142 E.J.F. Pickstock
143 R.R. Bowers
144 A. J. Standley
145 Margaret Joy Somogy
146 G.W. Hall
147 Alma Owen
148 R.D. Phillpott
149
150 Mrs Joan Anslow
151
152
153 G.E. Pugh
154 T.A. Rowney
155 N.E. Browning MBE MA
156 Philip G. Payne
157 Peter Atkins
158 A.G. Bloor
159 Stella Kidman Watson JP
160 John A. Lines
161 Paul Till
162 James McKenzie Went
163 John Wills
164 Anne Bayliss
165 Tina Martin
166 SR Katherine Egan
167 FR Cathal Cassidy
168 R.W. Wright
169 Mrs Lesley Bridgen
170 Charles Venables
171 A.T. Leadbetter
172 Walter R. Dean
173 C.R. Lester
174 Barber & Woolcock
175 R.F. Barker
176 Mrs B.S. Duff
177 C.O.L. Finlow
178 John Archer JP
179 G.M.J. Davies
180 P.W. Rogers
181 Michael Smethurst

Endpapers: FRONT — Speed's Town Map (1610). (WSL)
BACK — Plot's Town Map (1686). (WSL)